Meteor

action

By Glenn Ashley
Color by Don Greer & Tom Tullis
Illustrated by Robert Harrison

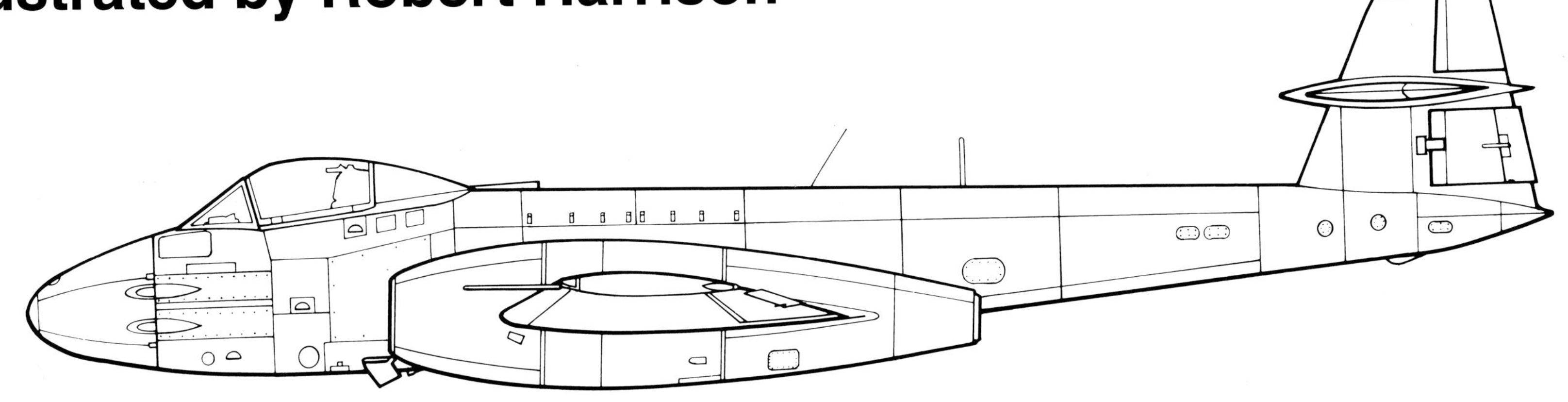

Aircraft Number 152
squadron/signal publications

Sergant George Hale of No 77 Squadron, Royal Austalian Air Force, shoots down a North Korean MiG-15 on 27 March 1953. For a brief period after the engagement, Hale's Meteor F 8, named *Halestrom* carried two small MiG kill markings, until they were ordered removed by the squadron commander.

Acknowledgments

I would like to thank the various museums, air arms and individuals who have been a great help in making this book possible. Without their help, it may not have been possible to bring some of these photos to light.

Credits:

British Aerospace
LT COL M Emonts-Gast (Belgian AF)
Air Attache, Belgian Embassy
Brian Pickering (MAP)
Weston Zoyland Research Group
J.R. Shore (Fleet Air Arm Museum)
Niles Herlitz (Flygvapenmuseum)
Adrian Gjersten
Israeli Air Force Archives
Martin Bowman
RAF Museum
B. Faux
Ken Slide
Nick Waters
Dr. David Nicolle
P. Davies
Antonio Linhares
Martin-Baker Ltd
Air Attache Israeli Embassy
B. Kedward
Larry Davis

ISBN 0-89747-332-9

If you have any photographs of aircraft, armor, soldiers or ships of any nation, particularly wartime snapshots, why not share them with us and help make Squadron/Signal's books all the more interesting and complete in the future. Any photograph sent to us will be copied and the original returned. The donor will be fully credited for any photos used. Please send them to:

Squadron/Signal Publications, Inc.
1115 Crowley Drive
Carrollton, TX 75011-5010

Если у вас есть фотографии самолётов, вооружения, солдат или кораблей любой страны, особенно, снимки времён войны, поделитесь с нами и помогите сделать новые книги издательства Эскадрон/Сигнал ещё интереснее. Мы переснимем ваши фотографии и вернём оригиналы. Имена приславших снимки будут сопровождать все опубликованные фотографии. Пожалуйста, присылайте фотографии по адресу:

Squadron/Signal Publications, Inc.
1115 Crowley Drive
Carrollton, TX 75011-5010

軍用機、装甲車両、兵士、軍艦などの写真を 所持しておられる方はいらっしゃいませんか？どの国のものでも結構です。作戦中に撮影されたものが特に良いのです。Squadron/Signal社の出版する刊行物において、このような写真は内容を一層充実し、興味深くすること ができます。当方にお送り頂いた写真は、複写の後お返しいたします。出版物中に写真を使用した場合は、必ず提供者のお名前を明記させて頂きます。お写真は下記にご送付ください。

Squadron/Signal Publications, Inc.
1115 Crowley Drive
Carrollton, TX 75011-5010

A Meteor F 8 of No 77 Squadron, Royal Australian Air Force taxies out on the Pierced Steel Plank (PSP) ramp of Kimpo Air Base Korea during 1951. The Australian Meteors were unique in that they were equipped with an ARN-6 radio compass in a clear housing on the fuselage spine. (via Larry Davis)

728

Introduction

The dream of jet powered aviation goes back almost as far as shortly after the First World War. Throughout the 1920s efforts were made to develop new types of aircraft propulsion using mainly rocket or gas turbine engines, but still requiring the use of a conventional propeller.

In the early 1930s, a young British engineer named Frank Whittle worked privately on a new engine design while still maintaining a career in the RAF. Whittle received mixed feedback from the various sections of the military about this new idea. A great deal of support was received from within the RAF, but the Air Ministry bluntly rejected his proposals leaving him to privately patent the project. His idea was for a gas turbine driving a series of enclosed impellers, rather than the normal propeller.

By the mid-1930s Whittle had formed Power Jets Ltd. to develop his new ideas from the drawing board to hardware. As this development continued, Whittle was busy trying to find a suitable airframe for development. In 1939 he met with George Carter who was Chief Designer at the Gloster Aircraft Co. .and their ensuing meetings developed into a firm belief that, a jet powered combat aircraft was not far away. Around this time, the Air Ministry did an about-face on their previous views and started to take an active interest in the project. This culminated in the issuing of a contract to Gloster for a new design to be used as a developmental airframe for jet propulsion, but also suitable for possible introduction into RAF service without prolonged modification.

The resulting aircraft was the Gloster E28/39 prototype, often referred to as the Gloster Whittle. On 15 May 1941, the first aircraft, serial W4041, made its maiden flight from RAF Cranwell flying for just over a quarter of an hour. The pilot, P.E.G. Sayer, was enthusiastic in his praise of the new aircraft on landing and the era of jet aviation in England was born. A second E28/39 was built, making its first flight on 1 March 1943, but some four months later, the aircraft was lost when the pilot had to abandon the aircraft in flight.

The loss did not adversely affect the program since the Air Ministry issued a contract for 500 aircraft under Specification F9/40 which called for a twin engined jet fighter for the RAF. Although originally requiring twelve aircraft to be built for development, only eight were built and the fifth of these, serial DG206, was the first to actually fly. This first flight took place at RAF Cranwell on 5 March 1948. Whittle's engines; however, did not power this aircraft since the WSB engines being built at the Rover plant in Coventry did not arrive in time. The aircraft was powered by de Haveilland H1 Halford engines. Apart from a few problems, including a nasty tendency to yaw violently at speeds near 230 mph, the basic aircraft was viewed as having potential for further development.

It had been the intention of the Air Ministry to start production of the F9/40 by mid-1942 and have the 500 aircraft completed by the Spring of the following year. This figure was later reduced to an initial order for 300 aircraft, now known as the Meteor, but continual delays were encountered due to production problems with the W2B engines.

Trials were switched to Newmarket Heath following the arrival of a group of Turkish Officers at Cranwell, but this airfield with its uneven surface was far from ideal for test flying, especially with a new and unproved power plant. It was during the tests at Newmarket that the yaw problem was rectified. The Royal Aircraft Establishment had suggested that the fitting of trimmer cords to the rudder might cure the problem. The cords were installed and they had the desired effect.

Not long after moving to Newmarket the trials team transferred yet again, this time to the Gloster company airfield at Moreton Valence, but also using the option of Barford St John. These allowed the company to use two permanent bases with better facilities and runways. These locations were also much closer to the company's main facilities in Gloucestershire.

Barford Saint John was used while Moreton Valence had a hardened runway built and, to keep the project as secret as was possible, Gloster had a separate hangar far removed from the rest of the base, which was used as an Operational Training Unit flying Wellingtons. Whenever the Meteors were flown, the local roads were closed by police, all other flying ceased and Very lights were used to indicate the start and finish of test flying. Most flights took place during times when cloud cover was low, reducing the possibility of unauthorized personnel seeing anything they shouldn't.

The next aircraft to fly was DG205/G, which was fitted with the original W2B engines. There were slight differences in the shape of the nacelles of the aircraft fitted with different engines, although this was only noticeable from the side. DG205/G flew for the first time on 17 June 1943 and was used to test the basic flying characteristics of the Meteor. On 27 April 1944, while flying from Moreton Valence, this aircraft crashed and was written off.

The next aircraft to fly was DG202/G which made its maiden flight on 24 July 1943. This aircraft was later used for deck handling trials aboard HMS PRETORIA CASTLE. This aircraft survived the war and is the only remaining example of the F9/40 in existence today.

Following the completion of the hardened runway at Moreton Valence operations moved to this location and on 9 November 1943, DG203/G made its first flight from the airfield. Once it had completed its test flying, it was used as a ground instructional airframe before probably being scrapped. Four days after DG205/G flew DG204/G followed it into the air. This aircraft did not last long, since it crashed on 1 April 1944. This crash, along with that of DG205/G later the same month, did nothing to halt or slow down the planned introduction of the Meteor into RAF service.

On 20 January 1944, DG108/G flew for the first time and by now the trials were concentrated on the less important design faults. One problem that was constantly worked on was the

The worlds first true jet powered aircraft was the Gloster E28/89 (serial W4041), which flew for the first time on 15 May 1941. The aircraft carried standard RAF fighter camouflage on the uppersurfaces with Trainer Yellow undersurfaces and the circle P prototype marking on the rear fuselage. (RAF Museum)

yaw problem and DG208/G was, at one stage, fitted with a modified fin and rudder to try and finally correct the problem. A little success was gained but nothing that would fully correct the problem until later versions of the aircraft. This aircraft was later passed to the de Havilland company as a trials and instructional aircraft.

DG209/G was used solely as an engine development test-bed by Rolls Royce before being handed over to the Royal Aircraft Establishment (RAE). Once they were finished with the aircraft, it was scrapped during 1946.

This left DG207/G, which had been built purely with the intention of fitting the de Havilland Halford H1 engine into production aircraft. Halford powered aircraft were to have the designation, Meteor F.2. Plans had been made by Gloster for production of around fifty F.2's but as de Havilland was developing the Vampire for RAF service entry in the near future, the company had little interest in the proposal.

The delays in development dragged on and on and it was not until 12 January 1944 that the first production Meteor F 1, serial EE210/G, flew from Moreton Vaence. The Meteor F 1 differed very little from the F9/40 except for the addition of four 20MM Hispano cannons mounted in the nose and an improved canopy.

The F 1 was powered by the W1B engines but these were now being built by Rolls Royce who could match the requirements for production. Before the F 1 could enter squadron service it was put through a series of tests by the Royal Aircraft Establishment. They were not overly impressed by the handling characteristics of the Meteor, and were critical of the performance and responsiveness of the controls. The Air Ministry, on the other hand, was now very keen to get the aircraft into service, possibly for the psychological effect having a jet aircraft would have on both sides in the closing days of the Second World War. This was doubly important as the Luftwaffe was not far from being ready to introduce the Me 262 into front-line service.

In some RAF circles the Meteor was considered no better than some of the piston engine types being developed such as the Hawker Fury and it was suggested that they be used as a training aircraft. The Air Ministry and RAF thought differently and by mid-1944, the first squadron was converting to the Meteor.

Fuselage Development

Gloster F9/40

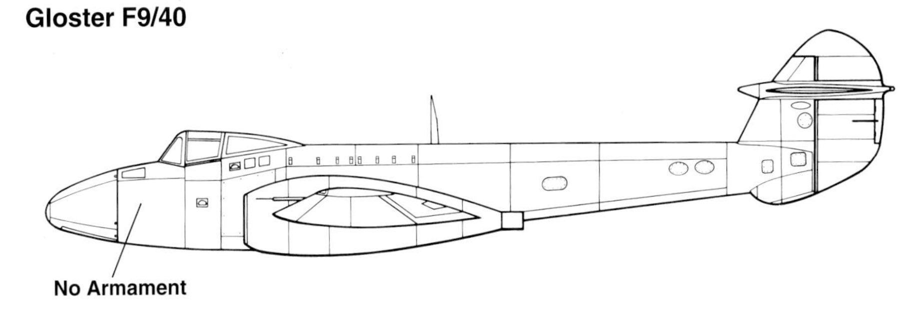

Meteor F 1

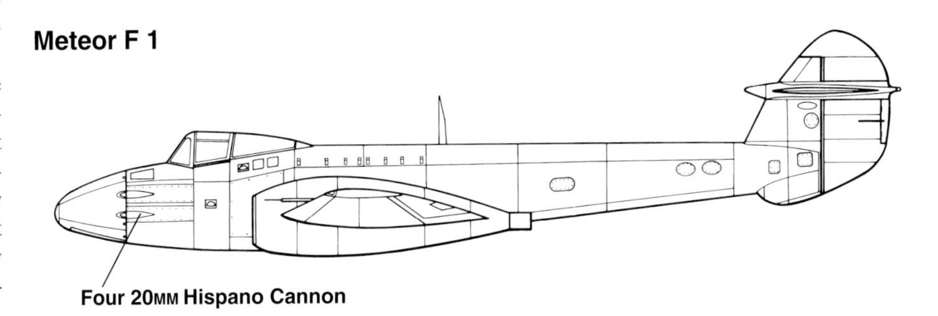

This Meteor F 1 of No 616 Squadron was parked on a Pierced Steel Plank (PSP) ramp during 1944 while its ground crew prepares the aircraft for another sortie. (Imperial War Museum)

Development

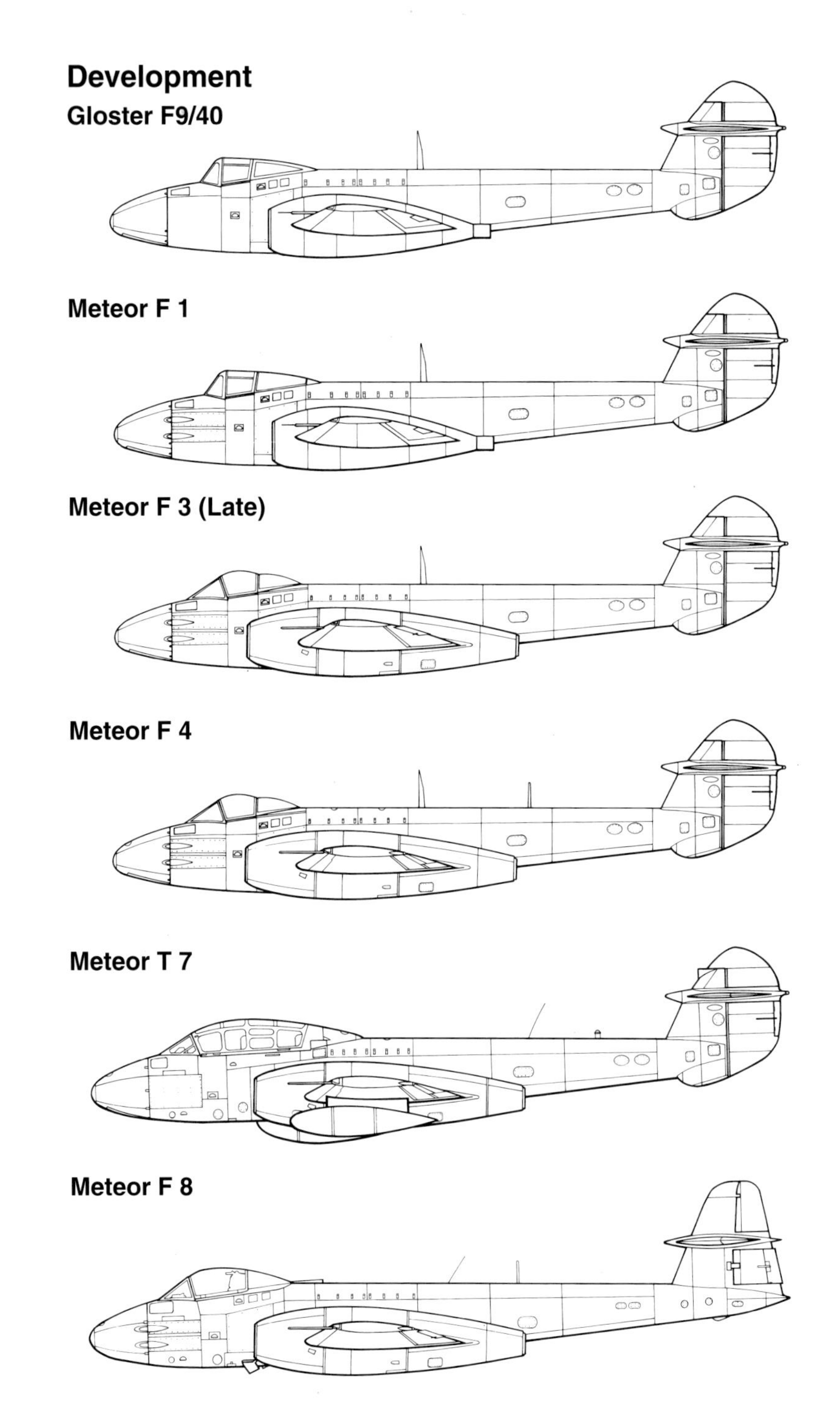

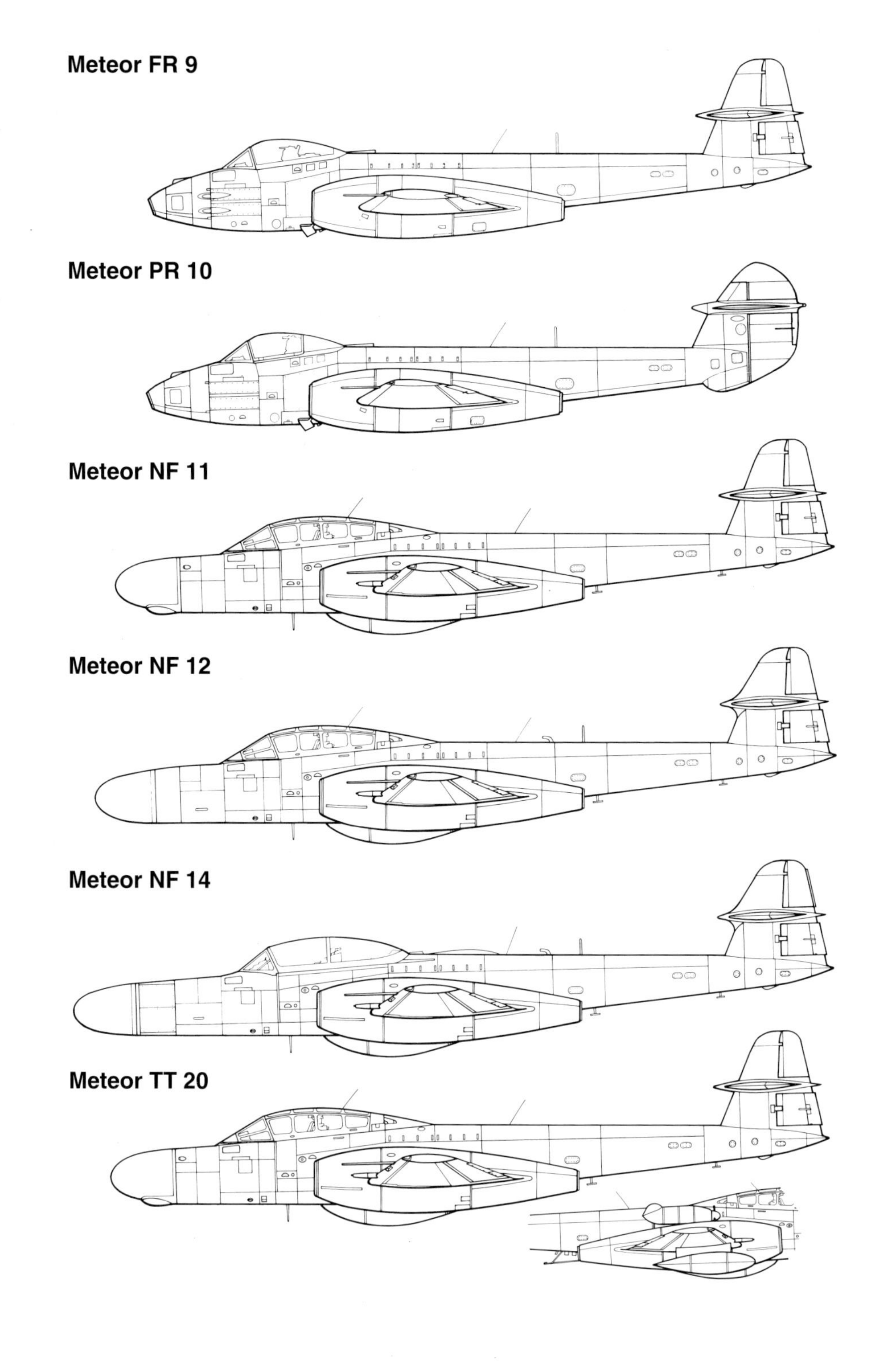

Meteor F 1 & F 3

The RAF had chosen No 616 Squadron, Auxiliary Air Force to be the first to receive the Meteor F 1. The squadron had just moved to Culmhead in Somerset and were presently flying Spitfire VIIs on armed reconnaissance missions over France prior to the Normandy landings and were under the illusion that they were to shortly receive Spitfire XIVs, little did they know just what was in store.

The new Commanding Officer of 616 Squadron, Squadron Leader Andrew McDowall, and five pilots received orders to report to Farnborough for a short conversion course, and it was then that they found out they were to be the first to fly the Meteor. The pilots found the transition from piston engined aircraft to jets quite easy, in fact, the biggest problem was the conversion from "tail dragger" to nose wheel aircraft.

The first aircraft, serial EE219, was delivered to the squadron, on 12 July and shortly afterwards the unit was on the move yet again, this time it was to Manston, which would be the squadron's home while they reached full operational status. By the end of the first week of flying the Meteor, over thirty pilots had successfully converted to the type, although the squadron was to receive only fourteen aircraft of the twenty F 1s built, the other six being used esablishhments for different tests and trials.

Initially the RAF decided to use the Meteor as a countermeasure against the latest of Germany's terror weapons, the V-1 "Buzz Bomb." Code named "Divers" by the RAF, these weapons were posing a major threat to the the British nation's morale, especially considering that the invasion of mainland Europe had just begun. The plan was for the Meteor to close on the V-1 from behind over an unpopulated area and using its four 20MM cannon, shoot down the flying bomb. This would obviously be easier than attacking a manned aircraft since the V-1 could not take evasive action when under attack.

On 27 July 1944, the first interceptions were made over Kent by Squadron Leader Watts and Pilot Officers Dean and McKenzie. Dean and McKenzie failed to intercept any bombs but Watts caught up with a V-l over the town of Ashford. With the V-1 in range and in his gun sight, Watts pressed the trigger button on the control column, expecting to destroy the target,but nothing happened. His guns had jammed at the vital moment and the V-1 escaped to go on and hit its target.

After this setback, it was decided that the patrols against these weapons would be carried out by pairs of aircraft, since the chance of the guns on each aircraft jamming at the same time was unlikely to say the least. The squadron's first success came on 4 August when Dean spotted a V-1 heading in the direction of Tunbridge Wells ahead and below him. Putting the Meteor into a shallow dive, increasing his speed to 450 mph, Dean got of a brief burst with his guns before they jammed. Dean then brought the Meteor along side the V-1 as close as he felt safe and with a vigorous flick of the control column banked the aircraft sharply. The sudden force of air rocked the V-1, unbalancing the gyro auto pilot in the bomb causing it to go out of control and crash harmlessly into the ground. This was the first successful use of the "tip and run" tactic by a Meteor against a V-1. Contrary to popular belief, the wing tip of the Meteor did not actually touch the V-1, since there was too much chance of damaging the fighter or even the loss of valuable pilots and aircraft. The crews used air pressure to get the job done, which proved to be an effective way to destroy the V-1 if their guns jammed.

Within minutes of Dean's success, the first actual shoot down of a V-l occurred when Flying Officer Roger closed on a V-1 over Tonbridge and opened fire with all four cannons. This time the guns did not jam and the V-1 was sent crashing into the open country-side. Over the next week two weeks, two more V-1s were destroyed as the pilots grew more skilled at stalking the small targets. A total of thirteen V-1s were destroyed by Meteors in one way or another and, although this seems like a small figure, it was a great boost for morale, both in the military and in the civilian population.

A pair of Meteor F 1s of No 616 Squadron on the PSP ramp of RAF Manston during 1944. The side hinged canopy was only used on the Meteor F 1. The aircraft individual code letter, Y, is repeated on the nose wheel door. (Imperial War Museum)

All of this exposure had made the Meteor the talk of Britain and any attempts by the Air Ministry to keep the aircraft secret would have been futile. In fact, the way the aircraft had broke into the headlines would soon be countered by the fact that the Luftwaffe was starting to put its first jets into operational service, the Messerschmitt Me 262, an aircraft delayed for several years by the political hold ups caused by Hitler himself.

The introduction of the Me 262 left the Meteor pilots anxious to deploy across the channel to engage the German jet in air-to-air combat. The RAF high command; however, stepped in and issued orders that Meteors would not be allowed to operate over German held territory. The officials were worried that an aircraft might fall into enemy hands. A short time later the Germans unveiled their next secret weapon, the Me 163 Comet, a rocket propelled fighter. At the sudden request of the USAAF and to a lesser degree RAF Bomber Command, No 616 Squadron was moved to Debden for a short while to allow USAAF bomber crews to adapt their defensive skills against the new threat, jet powered aircraft.

By this time the RAF was almost ready to introduce a new version into service and on 18 December, the first Meteor F 3 was delivered to No 616 Squadron. The squadron had, by now, moved from Debden to Colerne in Wiltshire. The Meteor F 3 differed from the earlier F 1 in a number of ways. The power plant was changed to the Rolls-Royce Derwent with a revised engine nacelle (although the first fifteen aircraft retained the Welland engines). The F 3 had a greater fuel capacity, giving the F 3 duration of an hour longer than the F 1. Additionally, the aircraft had an improved canopy and windscreen. The "car door" was replaced with a rear sliding bulged, bubble canopy and the windscreen was increased in size and raked forward. This new canopy greatly improved pilot visibility from the cockpit.

The introduction of the F 3 saw a change in attitude from the RAF high command, who now

This Meteor F 3 (EE35l) was assigned to No 1335 Operational Conversion Unit (OCU). The aircraft was written off after being hit by a truck at Port Said, Egypt during in 1947. (MAP)

A trio of Meteor F 3s of No 1335 Operational Conversion Unit taxi along the parameter track at RAF Molesworth during December of 1945. There are a pair of P-51D Mustangs parked in the background. (Imperial War Museum)

felt that the Meteor was ready to be sent across the Channel and into combat. On 20 January 1945, four of the squadron's aircraft were deployed to Melsbrook in Belgium to provide the base with air defense, but also with the intention of drawing the Me 262 units into combat. Despite a series of flights to display the new type to allied anti-aircraft gunners, the pilots still found the odd round fired at them during sorties over friendly territory and in an another attempt to distinguish themselves from the Me 262 and to provide them with a measure of Winter camouflage, the aircraft were given a coat of White distemper over the standard Dark Gray/Dark Green uppersurface camouflage. This soon weathered badly, giving the aircraft a rather worn and dirty appearance.

In March the four aircraft redeployed to Gilze-Rijen in Holland where they were joined by the rest of the squadron flying a mix of F ls and F 3s and it was soon decided to throw the Meteor into the middle of the battle. This was possibly due to the confidence gained by the advance across Western Europe and by the belief that victory was only a matter of time. On 13 April the unit moved to Nijmegen and four days after that the first operational sortie over Europe took place, a ground strafing mission against German transport near Ijmuiden. The Meteors were used mainly for armed reconnaissance missions, which had been the squadron's mission when flying Spitfires. Additionally, they flew a number of ground attack missions, but even with this activity, they did not encounter any German jet fighters.

On 20 April, as the Allies advanced into Europe, No 616 Squadron moved with them. For five days they were based at Quackenbruck, southwest of Bremen, Germany, before moving once more to Fassberg. These rapid base re-deployments caused problems. One of these was finding suitable landing fields for the jets. The squadron had flown from Pierced Steel Plank (PSP) strips or sometimes even grass fields, totally against the advice of the engineers at

In order to avoid being mistaken for German Me 262 jet fighters many Meteors were given an overall coat of White distemper as a recognition aid. This F 3 of No 616 Squadron is being manhandled into its revetment by RAF ground crews during early 1945. (Imperial War Museum)

Canopy Development

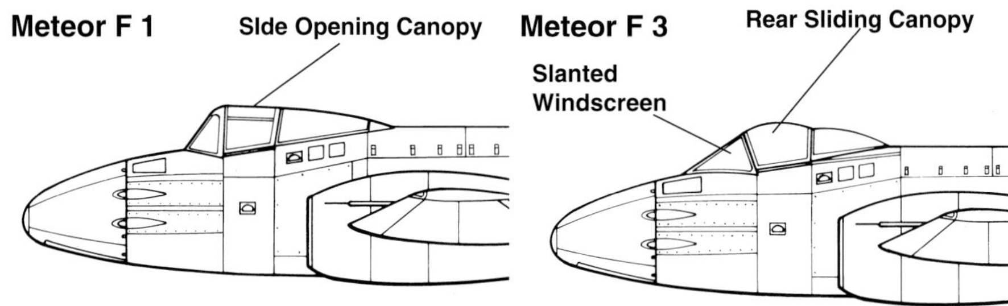

Gloster. Shortly after the move to Fassberg, the squadron suffered its first loss, when Squadron Leader Watts and Flight Sergeant Cartmel collided in a cloud bank. Both pilots were killed in the collision.

No 616 Squadron received a new commanding officer on 2 May, when Wing Commander Schrader took over from Wing Commander McDowall. The following day, the new commander led his first attack against a Luftwaffe air base at Schonberg, where the unit destroyed six aircraft on the ground. Other sorties were flown that day and a total of forty-six German aircraft were destroyed by the Meteors. The unit moved once more, this time to Luneberg. On 2 May, a Meteor pilot attempted to engage a German Fieseler Storch, but the more maneuverable German aircraft was able to avoid the Meteor's fire and land. Once on the ground, the Storch was destroyed by a strafing attack. As the war in Europe came to a close, the Meteor came very close to engaging enemy fighters at last. Four Meteors came across a number of Fw 190s and, as the British jets prepared to engage the enemy, a number of Tempests and Spitfires mistook the Meteors for Me 262s and prepared to attack what they thought were enemy aircraft. The confusion caused the Meteors to break off their attack on the German fighters. Shortly after this incident the war in Europe ended without the Meteor having the chance to prove itself against the Luftwaffe.

A month earlier, the second Meteor squadron had started to form at Colerne but No 504 Squadron would not be in a position to send aircraft overseas until July of 1945, when a detachment was sent to Lubeck to join No 616 Squadron, but the majority of the unit remained in England.

Following the German surrender, No 616 remained in Germany as part of the Allied Occupation Forces until they were disbanded on 29 August 1945. No 504 Squadron returned to England where the unit was redesignated No 245 Squadron.

In the days immediately after the Second World War, the RAF introduced more Meteor F 3s into service as replacements for slower piston engined aircraft. Of the post war squadrons, No 74 Squadron was the first to receive the F 3 in May of 1945 followed by Nos. 124 and 245 Squadrons in August (No 245 Squadron was a redesignated 504 Squadron). September saw No 263 Squadron receive the F 3 followed by No 222 a month later. Deliveries continued right through to July of 1948 when No 500 Squadron received its complement of F 3s, the last unit to receive this type. With the production lines switching to the newer Meteor F 4, the F 3 was gradually replaced in the front-line squadrons, but still lingered on for a while with the Royal Auxiliary Air Force, a force that was similar to the U. S. Air National Guard, in that it was a reserve force for times of heightened tension.

After its withdrawal from squadron service, a number of F 3s were retained for use in testing, but many ended up as victims of the scrap merchants blow torch.

Meteor F 4

Following the victory in the Second World War some semblance of normality returned to England for a short while. Before long; however, a new threat loomed from the East, in the form of an aggressive Soviet Union. In order to try and keep their technical advantage over the Soviets, the Western Allies pressed on with the development of a number of designs and improved ones already in service, including the Meteor.

The F 3 was now serving with sixteen front-line squadrons, but such great advances in jet designs were now being made that it became necessary to improve the Meteor in order to keep abreast of newer aircraft. Tests carried out at Farnborough by the Royal Aircraft Establishment showed that longer engine nacelles would improve the buffet effect and reduce drag, so new nacelles were designed that were slightly longer both ahead and behind the wing. Rolls-Royce was also developing an improved power plant for the Meteor and came up with a smaller version of the Nene engine known as the Derwent 5, giving the aircraft an improved maximum speed of 585 mph at sea level, a dramatic improvement on the F 3's speed of 415 mph. The aircraft also was modified with a pressurized cockpit and a strengthened airframe to cope with the extra stress from the increased power. With these changes, the aircraft was redesignated as the Meteor F 4.

The prototype F 4, EE360, was actually a modified F 3 airframe. The prototype made its first flight on 17 July 1945, but early tests revealed that further modifications would have to be made. First the wing was reduced in span by some two feet ten inches and the tips were rounded off, giving the wing tip a blunter appearance. The only drawback from this reduction was a slightly reduced rate of climb.

The problem of instability remained and it was decided to lengthen the fuselage of one F 4, RA382, by some thirty inches just behind of the cockpit. This modification had the desired effect. The change; however, was not incorporated into F 4 production.

With orders for almost 500 F 4s in hand, the production limits of the Gloster Co. were stretched and Armstrong Whitworth, who was already involved in the program as a major component supplier, was contracted to build Meteors at their factory in Baginton near Coventry. The Meteor was fast becoming the RAF's main first-line fighter aircraft.

The bulk of the early production batch of aircraft, with the shorter fuselage, went mainly for export orders or to specialized establishments or flights, but a handful reached RAF squadrons. 1947 saw the F 4 start to reach front-line units, with Nos 74 and 222 Squadrons receiving their first aircraft. At this same time the first export order was being prepared for delivery.

The Argentine Air Force had a requirement for 100 Meteor F 4s, the first fifty of which were diverted from aircraft intended for the RAF. The second batch of fifty being built strictly for the Argentines. The aircraft were based at Moron Air Base, with Grupo 2 and Grupo 3. The aircraft suffered from a low readiness because of the lower standards of maintenance given to the fighters by Argentine ground crews.

The aircraft did see combat during the 1955 Argentine revolution, flying ground attack missions for both sides. The Government forces used the aircraft to launch attacks against rebel columns and on 16 September, a number of Meteors attacked the rebel held naval base at Rio Santiago. The aircraft caused a great deal of damage to rebel vessels but one Meteor was lost to ground fire.

The same day the rebel forces captured Cordoba and at the local airfield they found three

A Meteor F 4 of No 209 Advanced Flying School is being refueled on the ramp at RAF Weston Zoyland during the early 1950s. The number 60 on the fuselage is an individual aircraft identification number and not a squadron code. (Westonzoyloand Research Group)

This Meteor F 4 of No 209 AFS made a crash landing on 12 February 1954. The aircraft ripped off the nose wheel and the nose cone when it hit a ditch after running off the runway. VT318 was written off because of the damage inflicted in this crash. (Westonzoyloand Research Group)

Argentina operated a number of Meteor F 4s with Grupo 2 and Grupo 3 at Moron Air Base. Initially they were given serials prefixed with the letter I (for interceptor). These aircraft saw combat during the Argentine Revolution of 1955, fighting on both sides. (via Nick Waters)

Meteors undergoing repairs. These aircraft were pressed into service, but without any supplies of aviation fuel, raw petrol was used. This caused the engines to overheat and on 19 September, one engine exploded, destroying the aircraft and killing the pilot. Following the revolution, the Meteor remained in service with the Argentine Air Force until replaced during the early part of the 1970s.

Deliveries to the RAF continued with No 266 Squadron receiving its first aircraft in February of 1948. This unit was followed by Nos 66 and 92 Squadrons in May and Nos 1, 56 and 63 Squadrons in June. By the end of 1948, Nos 245, 257 and 263 Squadrons had also converted to the Meteor F 4. With these deliveries came another export order in the form of an order from the Royal Netherlands Air Force for a total of thirty-eight aircraft.

The Dutch were rebuilding their forces following the Second World War and had chosen the Meteor to be their new fighter. They ordered a total of thirty-eight F 4s in a number of small orders, presumably ordering enough for each squadron as it re-equipped. The F 4 served with four squadrons of the RNethAF, Nos 322, 323, 326 and 327. Nos 322 and 327 were based at Soesterber, while Nos 323 and 326 Squadrons were based at Leeuwarden. The aircraft would give good service until the mid-1950s when they were replaced by another British fighter, the Hawker Hunter.

Around this time Gloster tried to pull off what would have been a major sale when they delivered two F 4s to the French Air Force test center at Bretigny. The French bought the two aircraft simply for test purposes and never followed up with an order for single seat Meteors.

In February of 1949 another RAF squadron, No 43, converted to the F 4 which was proving to be a popular mount with RAF pilots, who affectionately called it the "Meatbox." Only one more RAF unit would convert to the F 4 that year as a great deal of effort went into obtaining export orders. Two more European nations opted to buy the Meteor as part of their rebuilding programs. The Belgian Air Force ordered the F 4 as their standard fighter, purchasing a total

A pair of Belgian Air Force Meteor F 4s of No 1 Wing lift off from Beauvechain Air Base. The Belgian Air Force operated a total of forty-eight Meteor F 4s between 1949 and 1955. (Belgian Air Force)

of forty-eight aircraft during 1949. The Meteor saw service with Nos 349 and 350 Squadrons based at Beauvechain. Like the Dutch, the Belgians were more than happy with the Meteor and their F 4s remained in service until August of 1954.

Denmark was another customer for the F 4, placing an order for twenty aircraft to be delivered during 1949 and 1950. The Danish Army and Navy operated separate air arms which did not join to form the Air Force until 1950, so the first F 4s delivered served with the 3rd Air Flotilla of the Danish Naval Air Arm. When the Air Force was formed this unit became No 723 Squadron and the F 4s continued to serve with this unit. as well as No 724 Squadron, both being based at Karup. The F 4 would serve alongside the later Meteor F 8 with the last F 4 being retired during 1957.

The early 1950s saw even more F 4s being introduced into RAF service when Nos 600, 615 and 616 Squadrons received their F 4s. The following year Nos 19, 41, 500, 609, 610 and 611

Nacelle Development

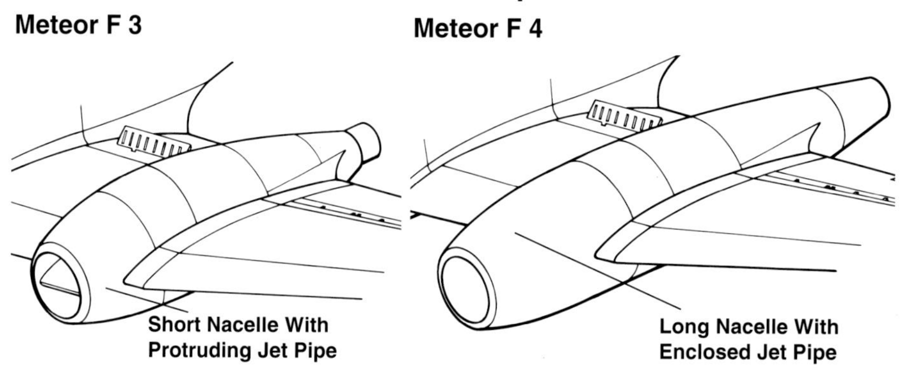

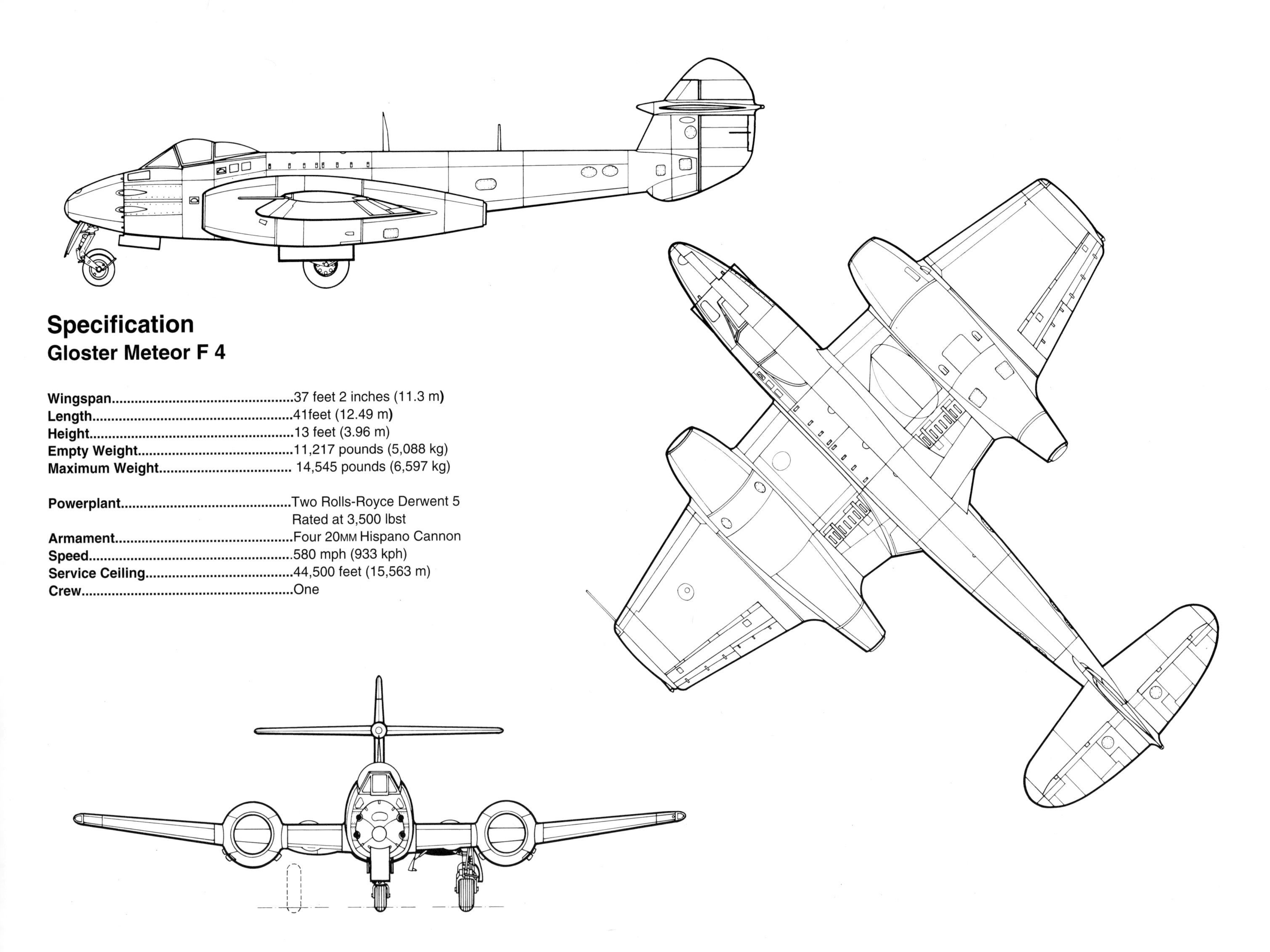

Specification
Gloster Meteor F 4

Wingspan..37 feet 2 inches (11.3 m)
Length...41feet (12.49 m)
Height...13 feet (3.96 m)
Empty Weight...11,217 pounds (5,088 kg)
Maximum Weight.................................... 14,545 pounds (6,597 kg)

Powerplant...Two Rolls-Royce Derwent 5
Rated at 3,500 lbst
Armament...Four 20MM Hispano Cannon
Speed..580 mph (933 kph)
Service Ceiling.......................................44,500 feet (15,563 m)
Crew..One

This F 4 of the Argentine Air Force, carries a Dark Green and Gray uppersurface camouflage over Light Blue undersurfaces. The aircraft carries a C (for Caza or fighter) serial (Gary Kunh via Nick Waters)

Squadrons came on line. One F 4 was loaned to the Canadian Air Force, but this did not result in an export order for Canada.

One surprise order for the F 4 came from Egypt, which ordered twelve Meteor F 4s during 1948. The delivery; however, was delayed because of an arms embargo imposed on the Arab states by the British government because of their war with the newly formed State of Israel. In 1950, the twelve F 4s reached the Royal Egyptian Air Force and they served until the mid 1950s when they were replaced by Soviet supplied equipment. Not a great deal is known about the operations of the Meteors in Egyptian service, but it is known that No 20 Squadron flew the type and was probably the only unit to do so.

The F 4 had a number of nasty surprises in store for the unsuspecting pilot, since the center of gravity could alter greatly in flight depending on the fuel load and amount of ammunition carried. If the aircraft expended its ammunition supply but still retained a large fuel load, the aircraft would became tail heavy. This could drastically alter the aircraft's stability in tight turns or if the pilot was trying to recover from a dive. Apart from these problems the aircraft was relatively pilot friendly if treated with respect.

The Meteor F 4 would continue to serve with the Royal Air Force and Royal Auxiliary Air Force until it was replaced by the improved Meteor F 8. The Meteor was to be used by a number of squadrons as the mount for their acrobatic teams. No 245 Squadron formed a four ship team in 1948 that not only performed in the UK but in a number of other countries as well. This team was joined by teams from Nos 19, 74, 111 and 263 Squadrons. No 263 Squadron became the Royal Air Force Fighter Command's premier team based at Wattisham. Unlike today's multi-colored specialized display teams, like the Red Arrows or U.S. Navy Blue Angels, the aircraft these squadron teams flew were drawn from the aircraft on strength and retained their standard camouflage schemes.

The Meteor F 4 was also used in tests aimed at the development of an air-to-air refueling system. Along with one F 3, two F 4s were modified with a refueling probe mounted on the nose. These were later joined in the test program by a number of modified Meteor F 8s. These aircraft worked with RAF Lancasters and Lincolns, as well as U. S. Air Force KB-29 tankers, using the probe and drogue method of refueling. Upon the successful conclusion of the trials, the aircraft were returned to their normal configurations and no more refueling trials were undertaken with Meteors.

The early 1950s saw the introduction of the next Meteor variant, the Meteor F 8, and in a number of squadrons these were introduced shortly after their first F 4s, which meant that the unit flew both types until the F 4s were gradually phased out of service. Other F 4 units; however, would continue to fly the F 4 until the mid-1950s when they began to exchange the aircraft for the Hawker Hunter.

Wing Development

Meteor F 3

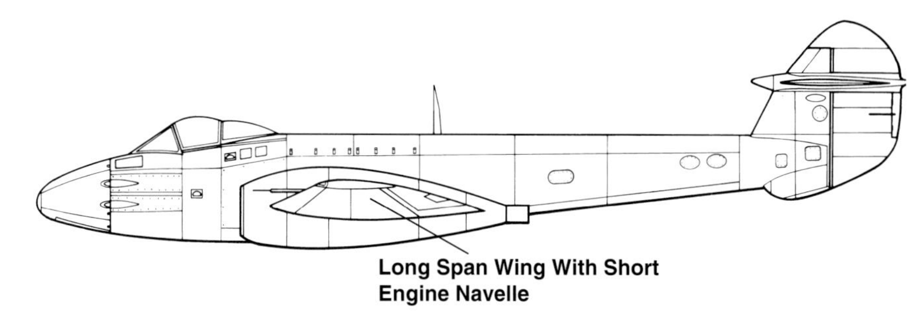

Meteor F 4 (Late)

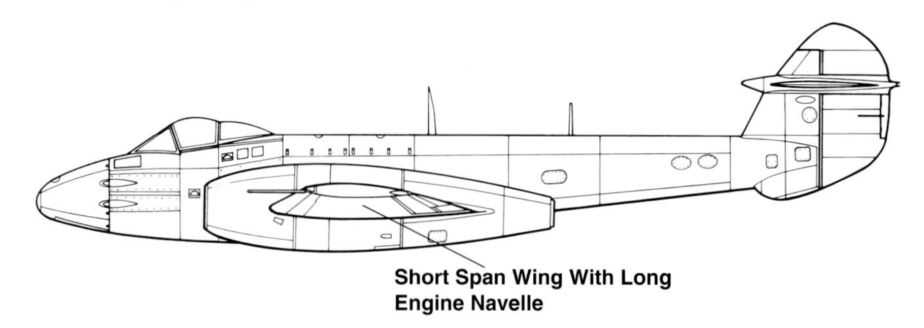

Meteor Trainers

As the development of the Meteor continued and interest was shown from potential overseas customers, the Gloster Company embarked on the development of a trainer variant to be taken on a sales tour around Europe.

A F 4 airframe was modified by removing the armament, extending the cockpit bay to house a second pilot and increasing the fuel capacity by adding extra tanks, including one external tank under each wing. After completing these modifications, the aircraft was assigned the designation Meteor T 7. The display aircraft was given the civil registration G-AIDC, due to it's being a private venture and painted overall Carmine (a shade of Pink). The prototype was taken on a sales tour of Western European countries and as a part of the sales pitch a number of foreign pilots were allowed to fly the aircraft. The aircraft was damaged in a crash landing while undertaking one of these demonstration flights with a Belgian pilot onboard. The prototype received substantial damage to the wings, tail and landing gear.

A second aircraft was built, G-AKPK, and this aircraft proved to be very successful. After this aircraft was demonstrated, the Air Ministry decided that the T 7 would be suitable for their needs for a jet trainer and an initial order was placed with Gloster. Eventually some 650 Meteor T 7s would be produced for the RAF and Fleet Air Arm.

The Meteor T 7 was not without its shortcomings. The RAF complained about the reduction of instruments in the rear cockpit, the inability of the aircraft to carry weapons and the unpressurized cockpit, all limited the types of training that could be carried out and limited the control the instructor had over the student.

The first T 7s to enter RAF service joined No 203 Advanced Flying School at Driffield in mid-1949 with the first course starting that September. A number of units received the T 7, ranging from Advanced Flying Schools to Operational Conversion Units to units teaching photo reconnaissance. The final total of RAF units was some twenty different units. The T 7 was a popular squadron or station hack and many squadrons flying other types maintained a T 7 for various duties. Others were used by specialized testing units. At the time of this writing, the RAF unit at Llanbedr in Wales still operated a couple of Meteors, including a T 7.

The T 7 was used by the Fleet Air Arm as an advanced training aircraft at various shore establishments from the late 1940s until the mid-1950s.

Export orders were regular, since overseas customers purchasing single seat fighters would usually purchase T 7s as part of the contract package. These were mainly used as conversion trainers since the Meteor was often the first jet type operated by the client state. Argentina was the exception to the rule and did not purchase the T 7 was part of its fighter purchase.

The first overseas customer was the Belgian Air Force which ordered forty-three aircraft between 1948 and 1957. The T 7 was used by all Belgian Meteor units for pilot conversion and as squadron hacks. Following on the Belgian order came an order from the Netherlands, who also ordered a total of forty-three T 7s beginning in 1949. The aircraft was popular with its crews with the air force being the main operator, although a number were converted to target tugs and ten were later transferred to the Naval Air Arm.

During 1949, the Egyptian Air Force purchased the first of a total of six T 7s they would operate. The T 7 deliveries would be staggered due to the fluctuating arms embargo imposed by the British Government at the time. It is believed that the T 7s operated from the same air field as the F 4s and other variants, under the control of No 20 Squadron.

A RAF Meteor T 7 (VW489) trainer of No 263 Squadron parked on a hardstand at Horsham Saint Faith during the early 1950s. The trainer later served with Nos 607, 63 and 25 Squadrons before being scrapped in 1960. (P. Davies)

Canopy Development

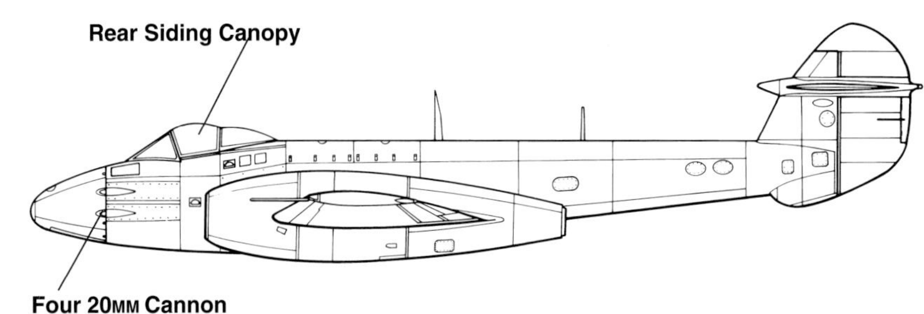

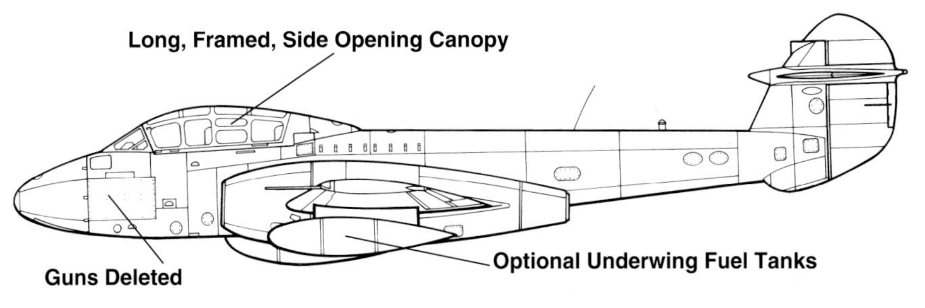

This Meteor T 7 (WA672) carries a lightning badge marking on the nose, which might indicate that it belonged to No 111 Squadron, although a positive identification of its parent unit is unknown. The aircraft was parked on the ramp of an RAF base during the late 1960s. (MAP)

In the early 1950s, a rush of Meteor sales to smaller countries occurred and these included a number of T 7s. Nine were delivered to the newly formed Royal Danish Air Force for pilot training. Two aircraft were sold as part of a fighter package for the Syrian Air Force and these are believed to be the first jets to enter service in Syria.

Israel was another customer for the T 7. Six were delivered as part of a package of different Meteor variants starting in 1953, five of these were built in Britain and one was built in Belgium. During that same year the Brazilian Air Force purchased T 7s as part of a package that included single seat fighter variants as well. In Brazilian service the aircraft received the designation TF-7 and the first of these were delivered on 13 April 1953. One rather unique item about the Meteor contract with Brazil was that the aircraft were paid for with a barter deal involving the sale of Parana wood and cotton to the British government, who would then pay Gloster. Some of these TF-7s remained in service well into the 1970s, in fact, the last flight of a Meteor TF-7 in Brazil took place on 7 Octboer 1971.

A few T 7s were delivered to other nations in small numbers or for trial purposes. Nine were delivered to the Royal Australian Air Force and were used for conversion training for pilots transitioning into the Meteor from propeller fighters. Fourteen were delivered to the French Air Force and these aircraft were used primarily for specialized testing with various weapons and radar fits at the Centre d'Essais en Vol (CEV). One T 7 was loaned to the Royal Canadian Air Force during 1953; however, this aircraft was returned within a short period.

There is little doubt that the Meteor T 7 played a vital role in training many of the jet fighter pilots of the period. It remained in service in many countries until replaced by more modern jet trainers, such as the Lockheed T-33 Shooting Star.

A flight of three Meteor T 7s of the Lossiemouth Naval Station Flight fly over a solid overcast during the mid-1950s. The aircraft are finished in overall sprayed Aluminum and none of the aircraft are carrying any identification codes. (Fleet Air Arm Museum)

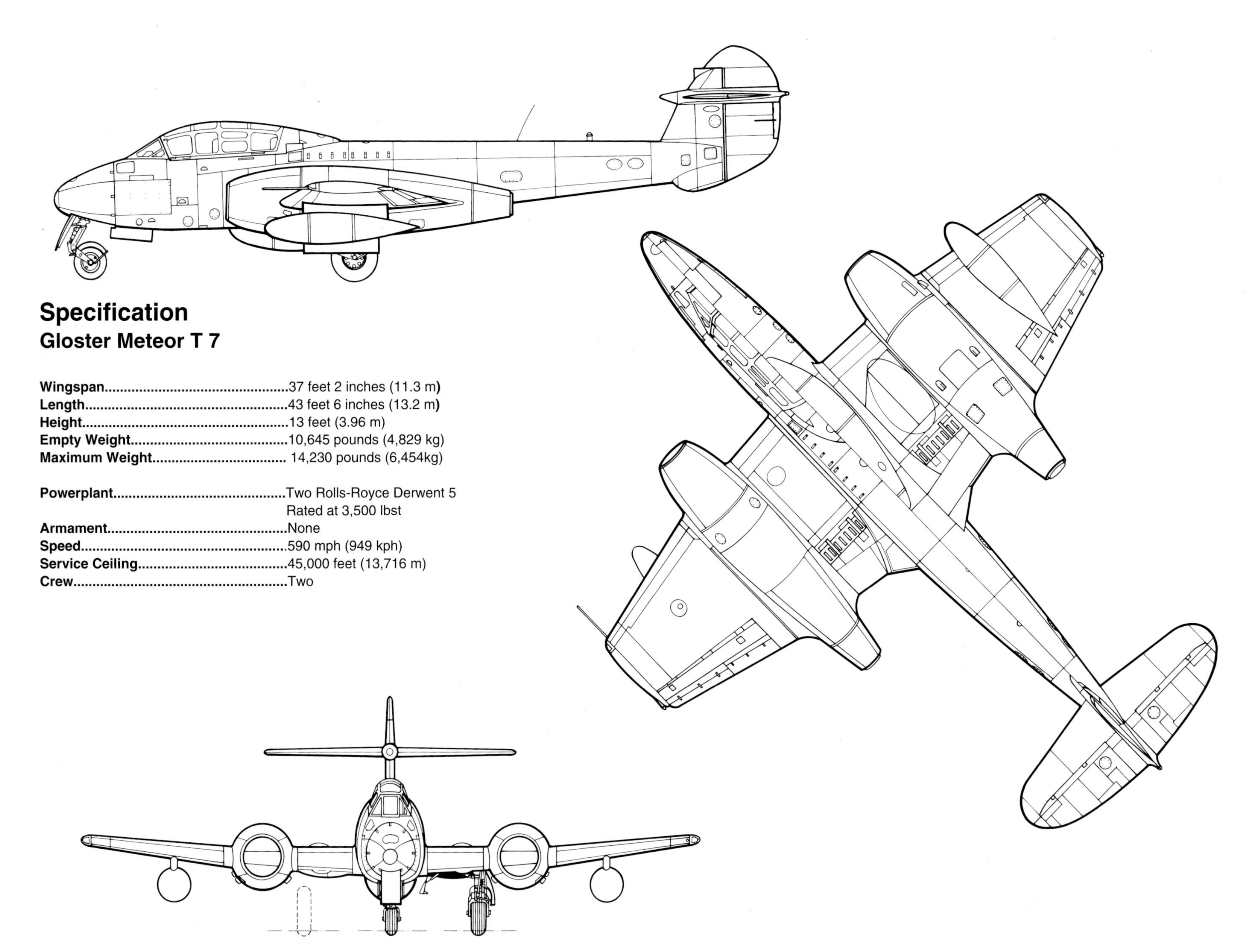

Specification

Gloster Meteor T 7

Wingspan...37 feet 2 inches (11.3 m)
Length..43 feet 6 inches (13.2 m)
Height...13 feet (3.96 m)
Empty Weight..10,645 pounds (4,829 kg)
Maximum Weight.................................. 14,230 pounds (6,454kg)

Powerplant..Two Rolls-Royce Derwent 5
Rated at 3,500 lbst
Armament..None
Speed...590 mph (949 kph)
Service Ceiling......................................45,000 feet (13,716 m)
Crew...Two

A Meteor T 7 of the Royal Egyptian Air Force probably on the Gloster ramp prior to delivery during 1949. The aircraft was finished in overall Silver lacquer with Black identification bands around the wings and rear fuselage. The aircraft's serial number was carried on the fuselage side, just behind the roundel in Black Arabic numerals. The aircraft was one of six T 7s ordered by Egypt. (Dr. David Nicolle)

A Brazilian Air Force Meteor T 7 (TF-7) banks away revealing the placement of the Brazilian star national insignia on the underside of the wing. Brazilian aircraft did not carry a fuselage star. The fin flash was Green and Yellow. Later Brazilian TF-7s had a radio compass fairing on the fuselage spine.

A flight of three Brazilian Air Force Meteor T 7, known as TF-7s in Brazilian service, fly over the British coast during pre-delivery testing. These aircraft have not had the colorful markings of 1st Fighter Attack Group at Santa Cruz Air Base.

A Meteor T 7 of the Belgian Air Force in flight over the Belgian coast during the mid 1950s. The overall Silver lacquer finish did not weather well and this aircraft was showing definite signs of weathering. The code ED37 is actually the aircraft's serial and not a squadron identification. ED37 was delivered direct to Belgium from Gloster and was not one of the twenty ex-BAF Meteor F 4s that were rebuilt to T 7 standards by Avons Fairey at Gosselies, Belgium. (Belgian Air Force)

Meteor F 8

In the F 8 variant of the Meteor, Gloster developed what was to many, the definitive variant of this classic jet fighter. The F 8 had a number of improvements over the earlier F 4, especially in performance and stability.

The Gloster Company had been concerned for some time about the rapid development of the Soviet MiG-15 in terms of the threat it represented and of the American F-80 Shooting Star in terms of sales competition. To meet both areas, Gloster used the stretched Meteor F 4 airframe to develop an improved variant of the Meteor under the designation Meteor F 8.

The Meteor F 8 prototype differed from the F 4 in a number of ways. The fuselage was some three feet seven inches longer and had an entirely new tail assembly. This new tail assembly featured a taller fin and rudder with a straight trailing edge, the aircraft also had a straight lower rear fuselage, giving the Meteor a much slimmer appearance. The prototype Meteor F 8, VT150 flew for the first time on 12 October 1948 from Moreton Valence. A series of flight tests were carried out by the RAE at Farnborough and the results of these tests showed that the stability problem had finally been cured.

A further two prototypes were constructed to test other modifications intended for the production F 8. These included the fitting of a new one piece bubble canopy (although early production F 8s had a metal rear fairing on the canopy), a Martin-Baker ejection seat and Rolls-Royce Derwent Mk 8 engines. The new engines gave the Meteor F 8 a top speed of almost 600 mph in level flight. Once these trials were completed, the Air Ministry ordered the aircraft into production.

During the early 1950s the Meteor F 8 became the RAF's premier front-line fighter aircraft and remained so until the introduction of the Hawker Hunter, even though the Meteor suffered from a lack of performance when compared to the American F-86 and Soviet MiG-15/17.

The first F 8s began to reach RAF front-line squadrons in the Fall of 1950. The first were Nos 1, 43, 74 and 222 Squadrons. In these early days, many units operated their new F 8s alongside the earlier F 4s until the F 4s were gradually phased out.

This Meteor F 8 (VZ482) of No 610 (County of Chester) Squadron, Royal Auxiliary Air Force carries standard NATO type day fighter camouflage of Gloss Dark Sea Gray and Gloss Dark Green uppersurfaces over Aluminum lacquer undersurfaces which was introduced during the mid to late 1950s. The unit markings were Black and White. (MAP)

Fuselage Development

Meteor F 4

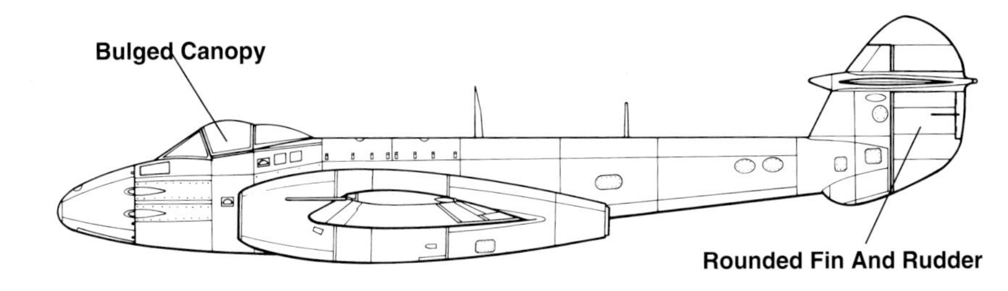

Meteor F 8

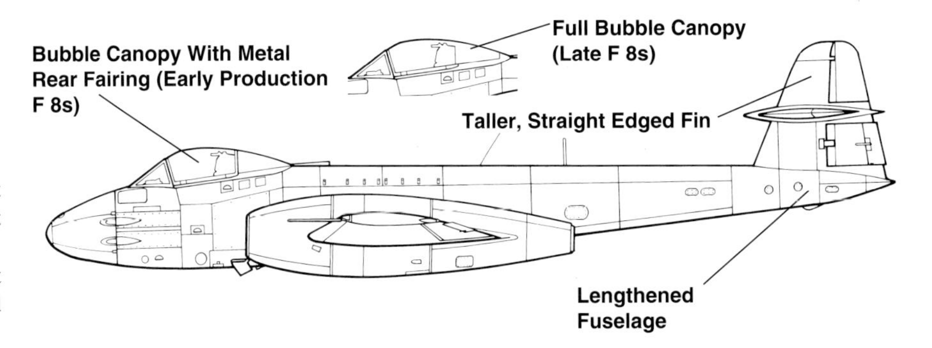

This period of British aviation was a color time when full color squadron markings were carried on the fuselage sides in a variety of patterns and colors. As a result, the Meteor F 8 was one of the most colorful aircraft to serve in the RAF.

Throughout the career of the F 8 efforts were made to improve the performance of the aircraft. Much of this effort centered around the power plant and trials with various engines. The main problem in getting better performance from the Meteor; however, lay in the now dated design of the airframe. As great strides were being made in fighter development, the days of the F 8 in RAF service was strictly numbered almost from the time it entered service. Within a short time, front-line units began to phase out the F 8 in favor of the Supermarine Swift and Hawker Hunter. The F 8 remained a vital component of the Royal Auxiliary Air Force until the disbandment of the service during the late 1950s. The "Weekend Warriors" of the AAF were pleased with the service reliability of the F 8 and the aircraft continued to serve with AAF units until 1957.

The F 8 was highly exported, especially to countries who were already operating the earlier F 4. The first overseas order was from Belgium who received a number of ex-RAF aircraft, but assembled the bulk of their 240 aircraft in Belgium. Many of these were produced by the Fokker factory in the Netherlands and delivered to the Fairly Avons plant for final assembly.

The Belgian Air Force used to F 8 to replace the F 4 in five wings where they served along side a number of Meteor T 7s. A number were also operated by various fighter schools and were also used for towing aerial targets. As with the RAF, the Meteor was gradually replaced in Belgian service by the Hawker Hunter. As well as building F 8s for the Belgian Air Force, the Fokker factory also produced aircraft for the Royal Netherlands Air Force (RNethAF). The RNethAF operated 160 aircraft with the first five taken into service being ex-RAF aircraft. The remainder were all built locally.

Seven squadrons operated the F 8 with the first aircraft entering service during 1951 and deliveries continuing until 1954. The F 8 gave excellent service to the RNethAF until 1956, then the first Hawker Hunters were introduced.

The third European country to fly the F 8 was Denmark which operated the fighter in fewer numbers than its neighbors. With the formation of an independent air force, the Danes ordered twenty F 8s. The first aircraft were delivered in 1951 at Karup Air Base along with a number of T 7s. The F 8s served with No 724 Squadron until the late 1950s and were the last front-line Meteors in Europe.

In the Pacific, the Royal Australian Air Force (RAAF) upgraded its fighter force by ordering ninety-four Meteor F 8s, with the first aircraft being delivered during 1951, in time for its use by Australian forces in Korea. As well as the aircraft of No 77 Squadron which were deployed to the war zone, Meteor F 8s equipped four other RAAF fighter squadrons in Australia, Nos 22, 23, 38, and 75 Squadrons. The F 8 gave reasonable service to the RAAF in Korea, especially in the ground attack role, but the air crews were quick to find out that the F 8 was outclassed in the air-to-air role by the Soviet MiG-15. The aircraft was replaced in RAAF service by a locally produced variant of the North American F-86, the Commonwealth CA-27 Sabre, although a few F 8s remained in service performing second line duties into the 1960s.

Squadron Leader Patterson was commander of No 247 Squadron at Odiham around 1951. He had his Meteor F 8s aircraft identification letter P painted on the nose wheel door. The aircraft has a commander's pennant and squadron badge on the nose just in front of the cockpit on the starboard side of the fuselage. (Ken Slide)

1952 saw the start of F 8 deliveries to two Arab nations, Egypt and Syria, although these deliveries would be staggered due to the on-again, off-again arms embargoes brought against nations within the region. The Egyptian Air Force aircraft were all ex-RAF aircraft, refurbished and resold to Egypt. These aircraft did see action against both Israel and the British during the 1956 Suez conflict. After Suez, the EAF turned to the Eastern Bloc (Soviets and Czechs) for their military equipment and the F 8s were phased out in favor of MiG-15s and MiG-17s.

Syria was a surprise customer for the F 8 and, like the Egyptians, their deliveries suffered from arms embargoes brought against the Arab states for their attacks against Israel. The Syrian aircraft were ex-RAF and a total of nineteen F 8s were delivered, beginning in December of 1952. Little is known of their service in Syria, except that they were flown primarily in the ground attack role with underwing rocket rails. The F 8s remained in service until the late 1950s when they were replaced with Soviet-made fighters like the MiG-15 and MiG-17.

The following year saw deliveries of F 8s being made to the Israeli Self-Defense Force/Air Force as part of a mixed package of Meteor variants. The aircraft were originally intended to be used in the ground attack role with underwing rocket rails, however, when first brought into service they were used in the air defense role, flying patrols along Israel's borders with its Arab neighbors. In combat, the Meteor F 8 scored two air-to-air kills over Egyptian aircraft. On 1 September 1954, two Meteors from No 177 Squadron on Quick Reaction Alert were scrambled to intercept Egyptian aircraft intruding into Israeli air space. The Meteors successfully intercepted the Egyptian Vampires and shot both of them down. During the 1956 Suez conflict, Nos 117 and 119 Squadrons employed their Meteors in the ground attack role, not losing any aircraft during the fighting. The Meteor remained active in IDF/AF service until

A Meteor F 8 of No 92 Squadron is parked on the ramp outside the squadron hangars at Linton on Ouse in Yorkshire during 1951. Later that same year the individual aircraft two letter codes were dropped in favor of a single letter code. (MAP)

The Belgian Air Force received their inventory of Meteor F 8s from several sources, including Britain, Belgium and the Netherlands. These six F 8s are all early production aircraft with the metal faired canopy. Later, Belgian F 8s were given a tactical camouflage scheme for fighter-bomber duties. (Belgium Air Force)

1961.

The Brazilian Air Force received the first of some sixty Meteor F 8s during 1963. These aircraft replaced the Republic P-47D Thunderbolt fighter-bomber in the ground attack role, seeing service mainly with Number 1 Grupo until being phased out during the mid-1960s.

The trim on this Brazilian Meteor F 8 was Red. Originally delivered with the metal faired canopy of early production F 8s, the Brazilian aircraft underwent a modification program during 1954, replacing the early canopy for the clear blown style. Due to a number of minor technical problems, the FAB suffered from a series of canopy failures of the modified aircraft, usually above 25,000 feet.

The Brazilian AF operated some sixty Meteor F 8s that served until they were replaced by French Mirage IIIE all-weather fighters. This Brazilian F 8 (FAB 4441) of No 1 Grupo carried very colorful squadron markings and the same squadron badge that had been carried by the unit's P-47s in Italy during the Second World War. (Antonio Linhares)

Little is known about the Royal Australian Air Force aerobatic team, the "Shooting Stars." It is believed that they were a Citizens Air Force unit flown by part time pilots. This Meteor F 8 (A77-875) had previously seen service with No 77 Squadron in Korea and was preserved at Williamstown Air Base. (MAP)

Korea

On 25 June 1950, North Korean forces crossed the border into South Korea, beginning a long and bitter war that would last some three years, without reaching a definite conclusion. As the communist forces pushed south, the infant United Nations put out a call for assistance from its member nations to halt the aggression from the North Koreans. Since the North was being supplied by both the Soviets and Chinese, a great deal of military assistance would be necessary to keep the country from falling under communist control. It fell upon the Western nations to supply the military forces to counter this communist expansion into Asia.

In response to the United Nations request for military forces, the Royal Australian Air Force decided to commit No 77 Squadron to the United Nations force. Stationed at Iwakuni, Japan as part of the Allied occupation forces in Japan, No 77 Squadron was flying the North American P-51D, but was scheduled to re-equip with the Meteor F 8 at any time. The unit deployed to Korea with its Mustangs until enough Meteors had arrived for them to begin conversion to the new fighter.

Once the first Meteors arrived in Japan, the squadron returned to Iwakuni to begin conversion. By the end of April 1951, some thirty-five F 8 and T 7s were on strength and the squadron prepared to return to the combat zone. The air crews had mixed feelings, since the MiG-15, flown by Soviet and Chinese pilots, had recently entered the war and it was well known that the MiG was superior to the F 8 in a number of ways. In a series of tests against a USAF F-86, the Meteor was found to be inferior in a dive and level speed, but it could outrun the Sabre and outclimb the North American fighter.

At the end of June, the unit moved to Kimpo, South Korea and a month later it was declared combat ready. Initially, the Meteors were used in the air-to-air role, a move that was nothing short of disastrous. On 29 August, a flight of eight Meteors were escorting B-29s in the Yalu River region, known to the pilots as MiG Alley, when the formation was attacked by six MiG-

A77-702 was a Meteor T 7 assigned to No 77 Squadron as a squadron hack at Kimpo Air Base, Korea during 1953. (via Larry Davis)

A Meteor F 8 of No 77 Squadron, Royal Australian Air Force on the ramp at Kimpo Air Base, Korea during 1952. The aircraft is armed with eight sixty pound underwing rockets and has a belly fuel tank installed. The clear fairing on the fuselage spine is the housing for a radio compass. (via Larry Davis)

A Meteor F 8 of No 77 Squadron, RAAF, taxies on the Pierced Steel Plank (PSP) ramp at Kimpo Air Base, Korea. After a short period assigned to the air-to-air combat role, the Meteors were switched to the air-to-ground role. For these missions, the Meteors normally carried up to eight rockets on underwing launcher rails. (via Larry Davis)

A pair of No 77 Squadron Meteor F 8s share a sandbag revetment at K-14 (Kimpo Air Base) during September of 1952. Both aircraft are manned and the pilots are preparing to taxi out on another mission. (via Larry Davis)

15s. In the ensuing engagement, one Meteor (A77-721) was shot down and two others were damaged without a single MiG being even hit. Some Meteor pilots felt that their lack of success was due as much to poor tactics as to the shortcomings of the Meteor. Most of the pilots in No 77 Squadron had been trained for ground attack and had little training in air-to-air tactics. Most felt that they should have been flying sweeps at the Meteor's optimum operating range, 15,000 to 20,000 feet, in order to take advantage of the aircraft's virtues (good zoom climb and acceleration).

Nine Meteor F 8s of No 77 Squadron begin section takeoffs from K-14 (Kimpo) during September of 1952. The aircraft are armed for a ground attack mission with underwing rockets. (via Larry Davis)

Two F 8s from No 77 Squadron taxi along the PSP taxiway at K-14. The PSP ramp and taxiways were hard on aircraft tires and the debris that collected on them was also hard on aircraft engines. (via Larry Davis)

The Meteors assigned to No 77 Squadron were very clean and did not carry unit markings. At this time, the RAAF marking was identical to that used by the Royal Air Force and the only way to tell a RAAF Meteor from a RAF aircraft was by its A77 serial. (via Larry Davis)

A77-134 taxies in after a ground attack mission. From the stains on the nose, it is clear that the aircraft has fired its four 20 MM cannons. (via Larry Davis)

Sergeant George Hale points to the name on his Meteor F 8 after his successful engagement on 27 March 1953. One of the ground crew has added the name "MIG KILLER" in the gun back blast soot. Later a pair of MiG kill markings were put on the aircraft, but they were quickly removed when the squadron commander ordered them painted out. (via Larry Davis)

Ground crewmen wait for Warrant Officer Bob Turner as he climbs out of his Meteor F 8 on the ramp at Kimpo Air Base, Korea. His aircraft carried the name *Elyane* on the fuselage in Red. (via Larry Davis)

It was decided that the Meteors would no longer fly close escort to the bomber, but would rather switch to the top cover role, hoping their presence would deter attacks on the bomber formations. This tactic met with mixed success, as the MiGs sometimes attacked the bombers by diving through the Meteor formation as if they were not even there. Occasionally, the Meteors did manage to get in a shot, and on 27 October, Flying Officer Reading claimed a "damaged" MiG-15, followed by Flight Lieutenant Blyth who also claimed a "damaged" on 2 November.

The first Meteor air-to-air kill came on 1 December, when twelve Meteors were attacked by some fifty MiG-15s over MiG Alley. Flight Officer Bruce Gogerly, flying A77-17, scored hits on a MiG-15 with his cannon starting a fire in the fuel tanks. The MiG was seen to spin out of control into the ground. A second MiG was also shot down during this engagement, but No 77 Squadron lost three Meteors. The last air-to-air engagement in which the Meteor met with success was flown by Sergeant George Hale in his Meteor named "Halestorm". On 27 March, a flight of four Meteors were flying a ground attack sortie when they spotted MiG-15s preparing to attack a USAF RF-80. Hale turned to intercept the MiGs and fired two rockets at them. As he turned to follow them, his wing man reported that he was being attacked and Hale turned into this new threat. The MiG attacking his wing man extended his speed brakes but overshot his target. Hale also extended his brakes, and was successful in maneuvering behind the MiG and a burst from his cannons sent the MiG down belching black smoke. Jumped by a second pair of MiGs, Hale engaged these and scored hits on a second MiG which began to stream white vapor. After his return to base, his crew chief painted two MiG kill markings on the aircraft; however, the unit commander ordered them painted out, since kill markings were, at that time, contrary to regulations.

Shortly after this engagement, the United States Air Force took over bomber escort and fighter sweep missions to MiG Alley with thier F-86 Sabres and the Meteors were modified for the ground attack mission. Underwing rails were added to enable the aircraft to carry either rockets or bombs. The squadron's first ground attack mission was flown on 8 January 1952 against the water tower at Chongdan. The success of this mission led to the unit being assigned a high number of attack sorties throughout the remainder of the war. The Meteors suffered a great deal of damage from ground fire since the aircraft had to be kept steady in order for the gyro gun sight to track the target properly. This was not the type of profile to be flying at under 600 feet with enemy anti-aircraft fire coming up at you. As the Chinese and North Koreans began to realize the limitation of the Meteor on its gun run, losses to the RAAF crews began to mount.

In order to give the Meteor some sort of edge to allow the pilots to get into the target fast and still get a hit, the Australians produced a modified rocket head which replaced the sixty pound explosive head with one loaded with napalm. It was hoped that this would get the job done on the first pass. This rocket head proved very effective against targets such as bridges and buildings.

By the end of the war, the RAAF Meteors had flown a total of 4,836 missions, destroyed 3,700 buildings, 1,500 vehicles and six MiG-15s. These totals were gained at a cost of thirty-two aircraft and their pilots.

Meteor F 8s of No 77 Squadron, RAAF, line the ramp at Kimpo, Korea. All of the aircraft have ground battery carts plugged in, giving the aircraft the external power needed to start their engines. All are armed with 60 pound rockets. (via Larry Davis)

A ground crewman prepares to pull the nose wheel chock from this Meteor F 8 of No 77 Squadron, RAAF named *Snooks.* The aircraft has the last three digits of the serial number on the nose in Black and the entire serial A77-134 in Black on the under fuselage fuel tank in Black. (via Larry Davis)

A Meteor F 8 taxies in past a U.S. Air Force B-26 Invader at Kimpo, Korea. This Meteor is unusual in that it does not have the clear radio compass housing on the fuselage spine. (via Larry Davis)

Meteor FR 9

Being a stable platform, the Meteor became an ideal candidate for the photo-reconnaissance mission, being far faster than the current generation of reconnaissance aircraft, Spitfires and Mosquitoes, then in service. Early attempts at creating a PR Meteor started with two Meteor F 3s were modified with cameras mounted in the nose section; however, these efforts were not proceeded with when one of the aircraft crashed and the other was sent to Farnbourough for trials work.

The Gloster Company continued to try to develop a fighter-reconnaissance variant of the Meteor and finally designed one that added cameras, but retained the four 20MM cannons. Originally, two F 4s were modified, one being re-designated as a Meteor FR 5. The first aircraft was used for test work on the actual shape of the new nose section, while the FR 5 (serial VT347), was lost when it crashed after coming apart in the air over Moreton Valance.

The next attempt came when a F 8 (VW360) was modified as a reconnaissance-fighter under the designation Meteor FR 9. The aircraft was modified with a new nose section containing a three camera window array using a remotely controlled F 24 aerial camera, while retaining the F 8s four 20MM cannon armament, the new nose section extended the length of the FR 9 by nine inches. Additionally, the aircraft was fitted with both ventral and underwing external fuel tanks to increase its range and endurance. The prototype flew for the first time on 23 March 1950 and by the end of July of that year, the first production aircraft were reaching front-line units.

No 208 Squadron, which was serving in the Middle East at Fayid Air Base, Egypt was the first unit to receive the type. The FR 9 was mainly used by squadrons serving overseas in the Middle East, Far East and in the 2nd Tactical Air Force in Germany. The FR 9 was a vital part of the 2nd TAF, flying armed photo-reconnaissance missions over West Germany and the first unit in Germany to receive the type was No 2 Squadron, which received its first aircraft in December of 1950. The unit was flying from Buckeberg and operated a mix of FR 9s and PR 10s until mid-1951, when they standardized on the FR 9. A second FR 9 squadron was also stationed in Germany. No 79 Squadron was based at Gutersloh and they converted during November of 1951. Both units would continue to fly the FR 9 until the introduction of the Supermarine Swift FR 5 during 1956.

No 208 Squadron was followed by No 8 Squadron, which was based at Khormaskar in Aden. The unit flew the FR 9 along side the deHavilland Venom during the 1950s, although in 1959, the Meteors became a separate flight, still under the control of No 8 Squadron. No 208 Squadron began phasing out the FR 9 during 1958, but No 8 Squadron retained their aircraft until 1961. The Meteor flight, No 1417 Flight, saw action against rebel tribesmen in Aden, while No 208 Squadron flew against terrorists in Cyprus, as well as flying operations in Aden.

The FR 9 was exported to three overseas customers, Ecuador, Israel and Syria. Twelve aircraft were sold to the Ecuadorian Air Force, being delivered between 1954 and 1955. These were all ex-RAF aircraft and were operated by No 2111 Squadron at Taura, remaining in service until 1972.

In the Middle East, good reconnaissance could make the difference between life and death on many occasions, so the purchase of good reconnaissance aircraft was considered vital to the air forces of the region. Israel, with its limited resources, had to buy aircraft that were capable of carrying out more than one mission, and the FR 9 was ideal in that it could be used for both fighter and reconnaissance missions. Seven FR 9s were purchased, being delivered between 1954 and 1955. These aircraft gave excellent service and remained in service until replaced by French aircraft.

Syria also purchased the FR 9, obtaining two aircraft which were delivered in the Summer of 1956. These continued to serve in the fighter-reconnaissance role until replaced by Soviet aircraft. Very little is known of their operations.

Ecuador also flew the Meteor FR 9, which were refurbished ex-RAF aircraft. A total of twelve (serials 701-712) were delivered during 1954-55. The forward portion of the fin was painted (top to bottom) Yellow, Blue, Red.

This Meteor FR 9 was formerly assigned to the Aircraft and Armament Experimental Establishment (A&AEE). Although officially listed as a Meteor F 8 it was fitted with a FR nose section making it a hybrid FR 9. (MAP)

Nose Development

Meteor F 8

Four 20MM Cannon

Meteor FR 9

Extended Nose With Three Camera Windows

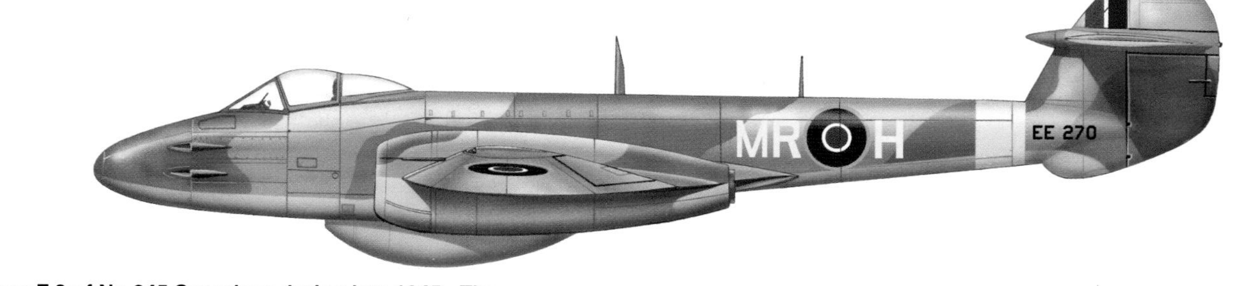

A Meteor F 3 of No 245 Squadron during late 1945. The aircraft featured long span wings and short engine nacelles.

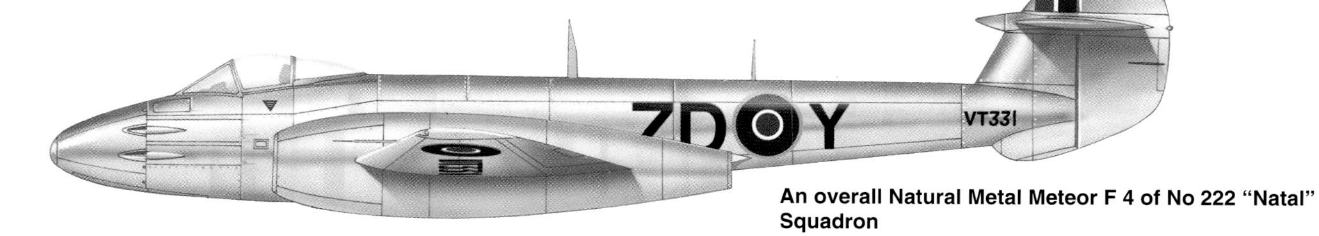

An overall Natural Metal Meteor F 4 of No 222 "Natal" Squadron

This Meteor F 4 was operated by the 1st Fighter Interceptor Group, VII Air Brigade, Argentine Air Force at Moron Air Base during 1949.

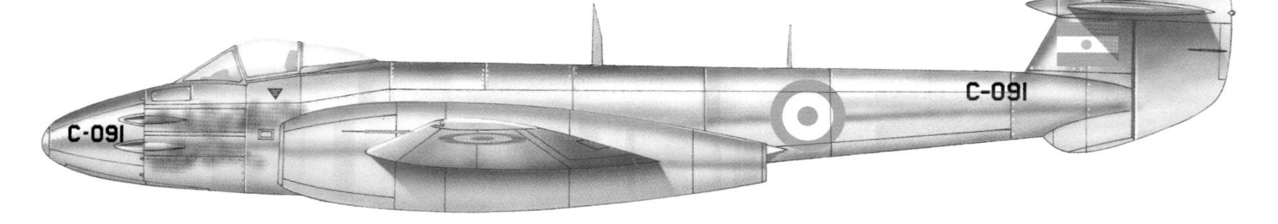

Meteor T 7 trainers were flown by a number of foreign users including Brazil. This T 7 was assigned to the second squadron of the 1st Fighter Group at Santa Cruz air base during 1955. The aircraft was finally retired during 1971.

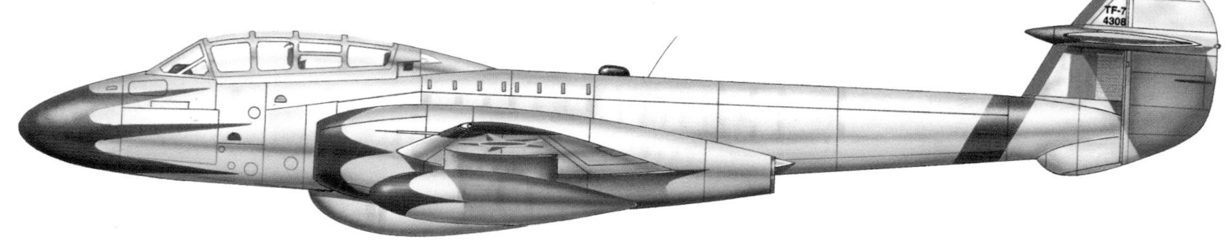

A Meteor F 8 of No 500 Squadron, Royal Auxiliary Air Force at RAF West Malling during 1954. The aircraft was flown by the squadron commander Squadron Leader Desmond de VIlliers.

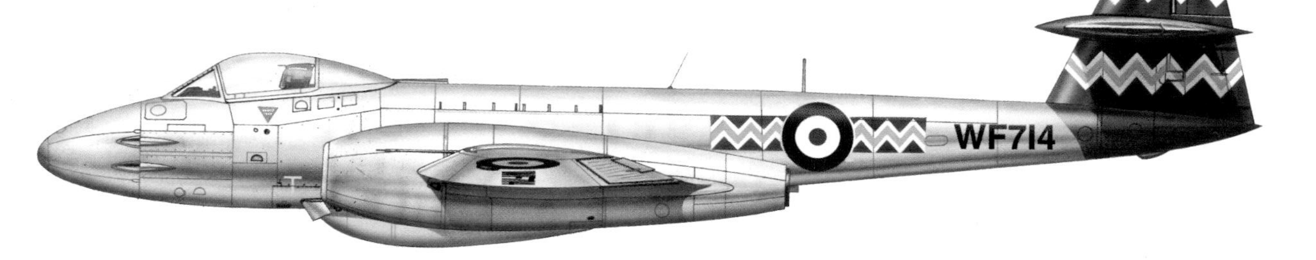

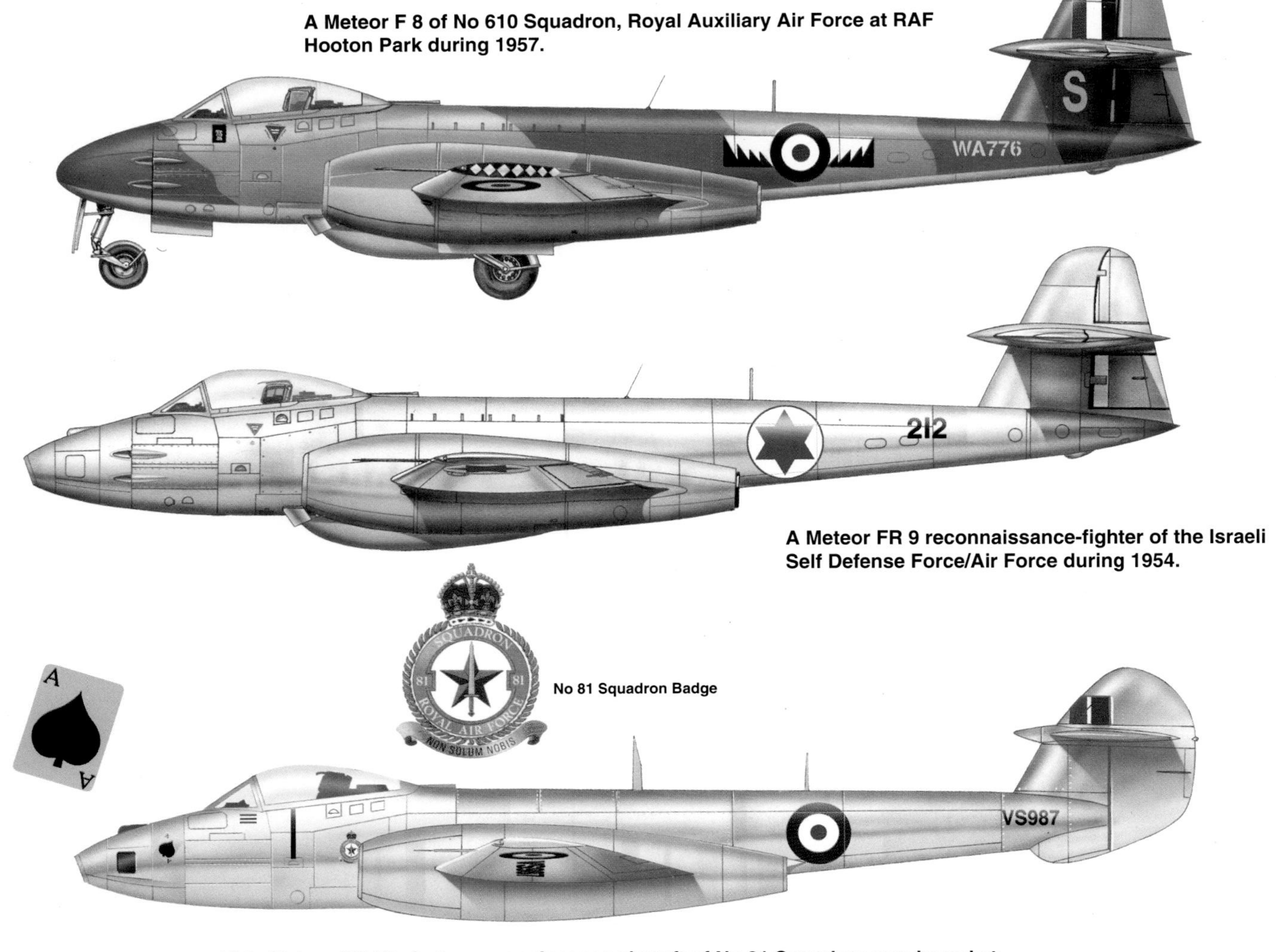

A Meteor F 8 of No 610 Squadron, Royal Auxiliary Air Force at RAF Hooton Park during 1957.

A Meteor FR 9 reconnaissance-fighter of the Israeli Self Defense Force/Air Force during 1954.

This Meteor PR 10 photo-reconnaissance aircraft of No 81 Squadron was based at Tengah, Singapore during 1960 as part of the Far East Air Force

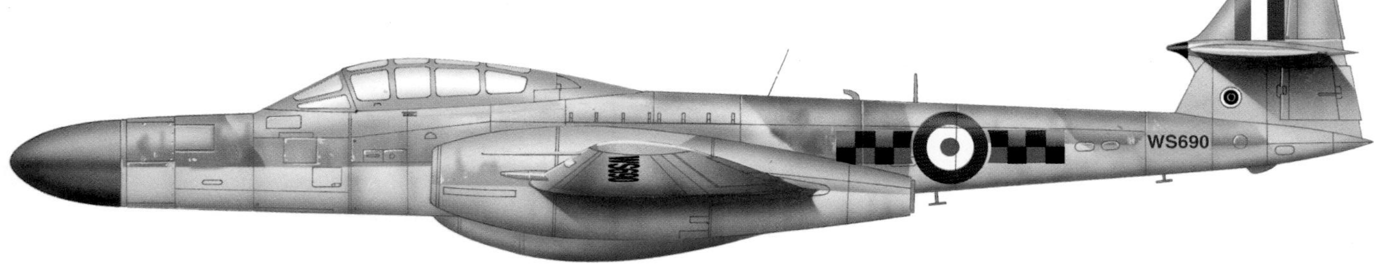

A Meteor NF 12 night-fighter of No 85 Squadron at RAF Church Fenton during the late 1950s.

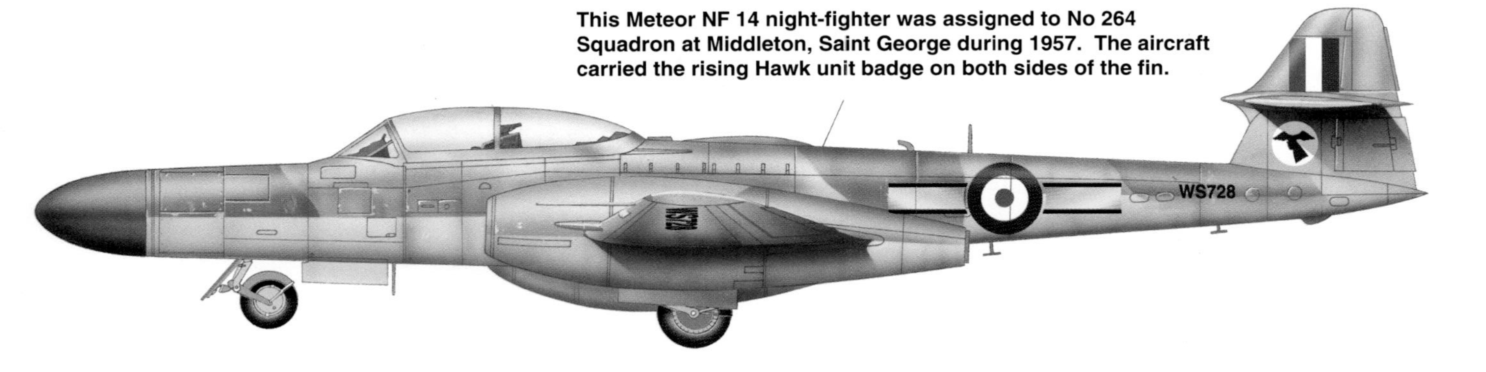

This Meteor NF 14 night-fighter was assigned to No 264 Squadron at Middleton, Saint George during 1957. The aircraft carried the rising Hawk unit badge on both sides of the fin.

Meteor PR 10

While the Meteor FR 9 was intended for low level, tactical reconnaissance missions, the next reconnaissance variant developed by Gloster, was intended to be an unarmed, high altitude aircraft under the designation PR 10. The aircraft differed from the earlier FR 9 in a number of ways. It was fitted with the same tail unit as the F 4 and had longer rounded wing tips. The armament was deleted and a pair of extra cameras were fitted in the lower rear fuselage as well as the one mounted in the nose section.

The prototype PR 10, serial VS968, was actually the first production PR 10 and flew for the first time on 29 March 1950. The first aircraft off the production line began to reach front-line units in December of that same year. The first two units to operate the PR 10 were Nos 541 and 2 Squadrons. No 2 Squadron flew a mix of FR 9 and PR 10s for a period while undertaking different types of reconnaissance missions over Central Europe. In June of 1951, the unit passed its PR 10s to No 541 Squadron, retaining the FR 9s. No 541 Squadron received their first PR 10s while based at RAF Benson in the United Kingdom before moving to Germany. The unit was based at several different locations including Buckenburg, Laarbruch and Wunsdorf before being disbanded in 1957.

No 13 Squadron was based in the Eastern Mediterranean and Middle East operating in support of British forces in the region. They received their first PR 10s in January of 1952 while based at Rayid, Egypt. A short time later they relocated to Akrotiri on Cyprus. They remained on Cyprus until re-equipped with Canberras in late 1956.

In the Far East, No 81 Squadron was the last RAF unit to receive the PR 10, with their first aircraft arriving in December of 1953. The aircraft were vital to British forces in the area, especially in view of the fact that there were several nations threatening British interests in the area. The PR 10s remained active until finally replaced by reconnaissance variants of the Canberra. This phase out began during 1958, but the PR 10 would not totally be replaced until July of 1961.

The Meteor had proven itself to be a worthy PR aircraft, which was able to undertake this mission with success. With the introduction of faster, higher flying aircraft the PR 10 was rapidly phased out, especially in areas where the threat of surface-to-air missiles (SAMs) was beginning to become apparent.

Due to its specialized nature, the PR 10 was not a viable candidate for export and none were used by foreign nations.

This Meteor PR 10 (WB167) was intended to see service with the Far East Air Force, but with the RAF's withdrawal from certain areas, the aircraft became surplus. It was sent fresh from the factory to a storage yard and later scrapped during March of 1960. (MAP)

Fuselage Development

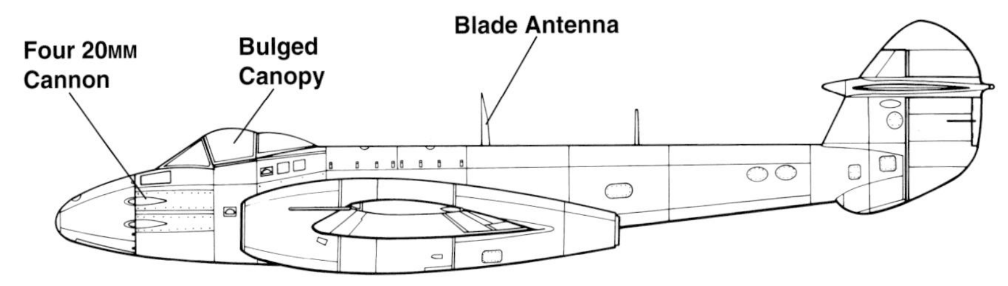

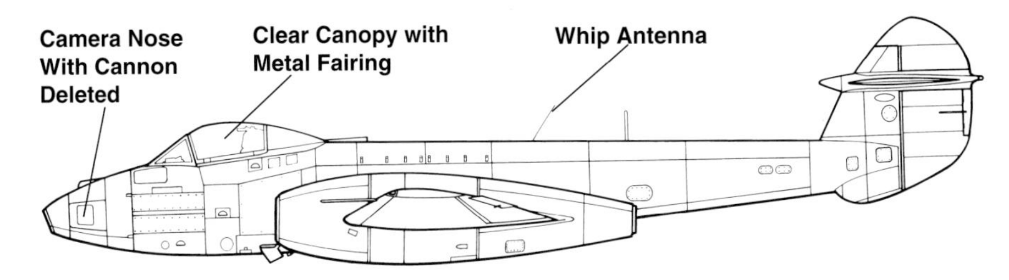

This PR 10 (VW379) still carries the markings of the last unit it served with, No 541 Squadron. The aircraft was placed in long term open storage once it was withdrawn from active service. It was finished in Light Gray on the upper surfaces with PRU Blue undersurfaces. (MAP)

Meteor NF 11

From late in the Second World War until the early 1950s the RAF's main night-fighter had been the deHavilland Mosquito, which although having been an excellent choice, could not serve forever and a replacement was urgently needed.

The Meteor was an ideal choice for development as a night-fighter, since it was faster than most bombers of the era and speed would not be as important as a stable weapons platform in the darkness of night, especially considering the relative newness of airborne radar.

A number of designs had been put to the Air Ministry, but all had failed to generate sufficient interest to warrant a production order. Gloster was working on a long term project (that would evolve as the Javelin) but what was needed was a interim aircraft to take over from the Mosquito until this was ready for service.

As a result, Gloster proposed production of a two seat Meteor with a radar set mounted in the nose. With Gloster committed to the Javelin project, the Armstrong Whitworth Company was selected to built the night-fighter variants of the Meteor. Armstrong Whitworth was no stranger to the Meteor, having built Meteors during the latter part of the Second World War.

Following trials with a modified T 7, the prototype night-fighter, designated the NF 11, was flown for the first time on 31 May 1950. The aircraft had a number of features from different Meteor variants. It had the center and rear fuselage of a F 8, a Meteor T 7 canopy, the longer wings and rounded wing tips of a PR 10 along with a new nose which was longer and more bulbous. This nose housed the Mk 10 Air Intercept (AI) radar. The armament was moved from the nose to the wings outboard of the engine nacelles and the aircraft was given increased fuel tankage to increase its endurance.

The first NF 11s began reaching RAF units during mid-1951, starting with No 29 Squadron,

The prototype Meteor NF II (WA546) night-fighter was really a hybrid aircraft that featured different items from earlier versions of the Meteor. It had a F 8 fuselage, PR 10 wings, and a T 7 style canopy. The nose section was lengthened to house a Mk 10 Air Intercept radar. The aircraft carries the Yellow circle and P identifying it as a prototype for testing at Farnborough. (MAP)

Fuselage Development

Meteor F 8

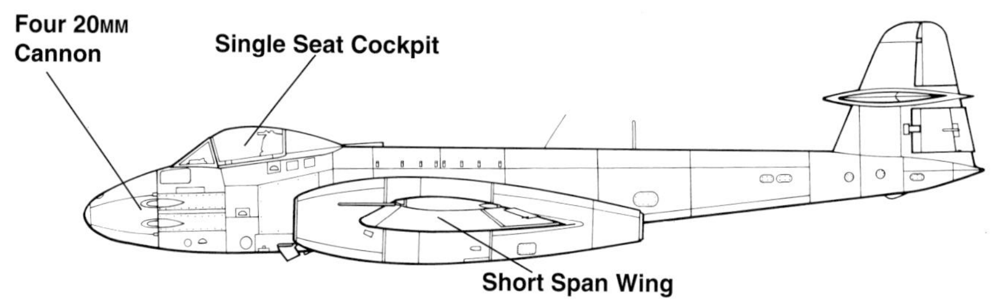

Meteor NF 11

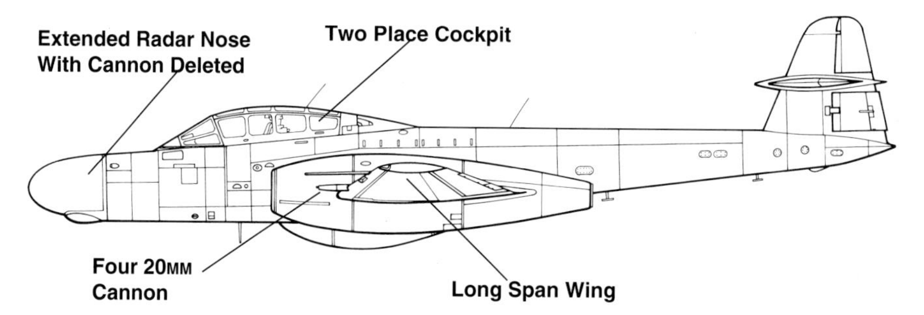

which was followed shortly by Nos 141 and 85 Squadrons. The next year saw additional squadrons re-equip with the NF 11 with deliveries continuing until 1955, when No 125 Squadron received their aircraft. In 1959, Nos 68 and 256 Squadrons were renumbered as Nos 5 and 11 Squadrons, respectively.

The NF 11, while not a remarkable aircraft, served as a very reliable night-fighter, especially when it was originally envisioned as only a stop-gap. A few RAF NF 11 squadrons operated their Meteors as composite units along side the Vampire NF 11s and later with Venom NF 2 and 3.

There were problems with the underwing tanks, which tended to collapse during high speed flight or when the wing cannons were fired. A number of tests were conducted to try to strengthen these through pressurization, but these met with little success. The heavily framed canopy also caused problems for crews, making night landings difficult at best.

Apart from the RAF a number of overseas customers also operated the NF 11. The first two were Belgium and Denmark which both received their first aircraft during 1952. Belgium received twelve ex-RAF aircraft with a further twelve ex-RAF aircraft delivered during 1956. The aircraft remained in service until they were replaced during 1958. A number of these operated with a Belgian serial on the fuselage, while others retained their RAF serials under the wings. This surely must have caused some confusion to other pilots. The Meteor NF 11 served with Nos 10 and 11 Squadrons, until they were phased out in favor of the Avro CF-100.

Denmark received twenty NF 11s during 1952-53 direct from Armstrong-Whitworth. These

aircraft were serialed 501 to 520 and were operational with No 723 Squadron at Karup covering NATO's northern flank until they were replaced by F-86s during 1958.

The most surprising customer for the NF 11 was France. Some forty-one examples of the NF 11 were delivered to France during 1954-55, all ex-RAF aircraft. A small number were delivered to the CEV for test purposes, while the remainder went into service with EC30, the first jet night-fighter unit in the French Air Force. A number of aircraft from this unit would see service in Algeria before being replaced by the Vatour IIN during the late 1950s. A number of CEV aircraft remained in service until the mid-1980s, conducting various test programs.

Only one other NF 11 was known to have been sent overseas. One aircraft was delivered to the Royal Australian Air Force during 1953, receiving the serial A77-3.

(Left) No 29 Squadron, based at RAF Tangmere, was the first RAF unit to re-equip with the Meteor NF 11 night-fighter during August of 1951. This Meteor NF 11 (WM174) carries the individual aircraft code L on the fin and full squadron markings. The markings consist of Red and White bars, each with three Red Xs. (MAP)

This Meteor NF 11 (WM151), taxiing in at RAF Stradishall during the early 1950s, is unusual in that it has the nose radome painted in camouflage colors. Normally, NF 11s had the nose radome painted in Black. (MAP)

The Empire Test Pilots School (ETPS) has flown just about every type of aircraft that has served with the RAF. This Meteor NF 11 (WD769) served with the ETPS during the 1950s and carries the ETPS name on the nose under the windscreen. (MAP)

This very weathered Meteor NF 11 (WD668) still carries the markings of its last active unit, No 5 Squadron. The aircraft was in open storage during 1961. The Meteor NF 11 was the first Meteor variant to carry its cannon armament in the wings. (MAP)

A total of twenty-four Meteor NF 11s were flown by the Belgian Air Force. The radome on this aircraft appears to be painted Black on the upper side. The aircraft has the individual aircraft code letter, H, repeated on the nose wheel door. (Belgian Air Force)

A Belgian Air Force NF 11 sits in the middle of the snowbound airfield at Beauvechain. This aircraft was assigned to No 10 Squadron of No 1 Wing and retained RAF camouflage. Some Belgian NF 11s also retained RAF serials under the wings. (Belgian Air Force)

Meteor NF 12

As development of newer radars progressed, Armstrong-Whitworth proposed a new variant of the Meteor night-fighter to take advantage of the new radar. This aircraft, designated the NF 12 differed from the earlier NF 11 in a number of ways. The most noticeable, was the extended nose cone that housed a new radar, an American APS-21. In order to house this new radar, the nose was extended by seventeen inches. This altered the center of gravity of the aircraft and to rectify this problem, the fin area was enlarged. The aircraft also incorporated new Derwent 9 engines each with an extra 100 pounds of thrust. This added thrust did not affect the aircraft's speed, but it did require the strengthening of the wing structure.

The prototype NF 12 flew for the first time on 21 April 1953 and when production ceased, some 100 aircraft had been produced. All of these would be operated by seven RAF squadrons, the NF 12 not being exported to any overseas customers.

The first unit to receive the NF 12 was No 85 Squadron, which received their first aircraft in August of 1953 at RAF West Malling. The following year, the unit also received the first of the follow-on NF 14, both types being operated together throughout the mid-1950s. This was a practice followed by several other squadrons during this period.

During 1954, three more units equipped with the NF 12 as their main aircraft, these being Nos 25 (January), 152 (June) and 46 (August) with Nos 72 and 153 following during 1955 and finally No 64 in September of 1956.

Several of the units moved bases to the North of England as they re-equipped with night-fighters, since it was felt that the threat would come from Soviet bombers flying around the top of Scandinavia. This move was important due to the fact that the response time would be

Fuselage Development

Meteor NF 11

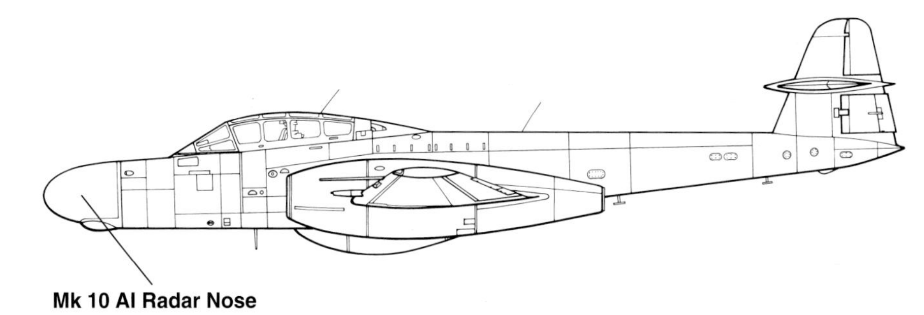

Meteor NF 12

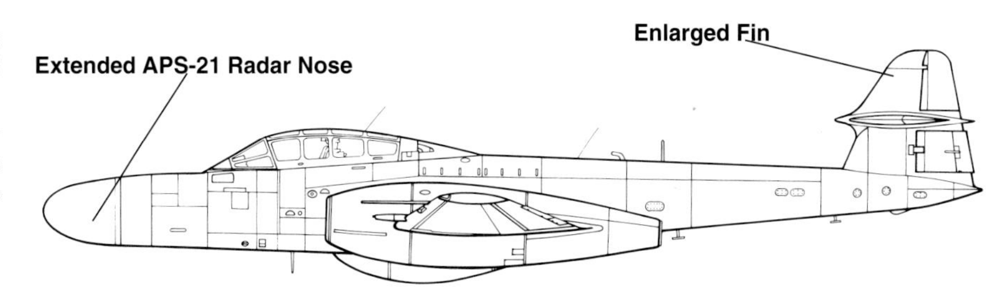

This Meteor NF 12 (WS665) of No 25 Squadron has a tow bar attached to the nose wheel. The unit was based at West Malling during the mid-1950s. The squadron markings consisted of Silver and Black bars and a unit badge on the fin. (MAP)

A Meteor NF 12 (WS607) of No 72 Squadron taxies in on a typical British summer day, wet. The aircraft was based at RAF Church Fenten during 1956. (MAP)

fairly short and the aircraft would still have to get in close to any target to engage it with their four 20MM cannon.

Throughout the height of the Cold War, these aircraft would remain a vital part of the United Kingdom's air defense, until the latter part of the 1950s. NF 12s began to be phased out and replaced by Javelins as early as February of 1956, when No 46 Squadron started its re-equipment program, although the bulk of its aircraft were not replaced until 1958. Nos 25 and 72 Squadrons, did not relinquish their aircraft until early 1959, ending the career of the NF 12 in RAF service.

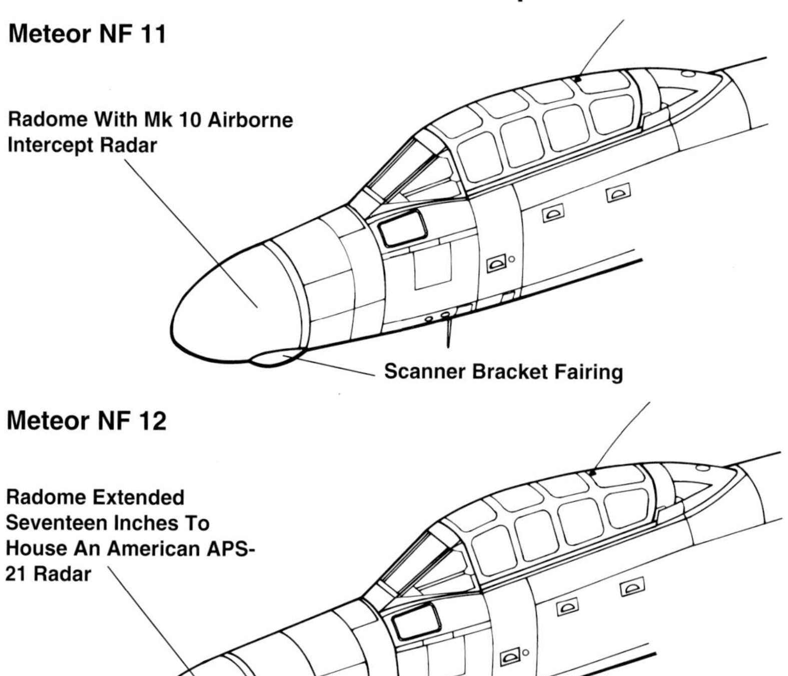

Three Meteor NF 12s of the All Weather Operational Conversion Unit on the flightline at RAF West Raynham, with WS615/F in the foreground. This was just one of several All Weather units based there as part of the Central Fighter Establishment. (MAP)

Ground crewmen perform maintenance on the radar, as other crewmen refuel this Meteor NF 12 (WS604) of No 64 Squadron on the ramp at RAF Middleton Saint George during 1957. (MAP)

Meteor NF 13

Although numerically later than the NF 12, the NF 13 was available before it. The NF 13 was, in fact, nothing more than a tropicalized variant of the NF 11 intended for use by the RAF in the Middle East and only a small number of this variant was produced.

The prototype flew for the first time on 23 December 1952. After completing its flight tests, this aircraft was later delivered to No 39 Squadron. The main difference between the NF 11 and NF 13 included the installation of cold air ducts on the lower fuselage, for cockpit cooling in tropical climates. Other modifications included the installation of Distance Measuring Equipment (DME), a radio compass and (on some aircraft) larger flaps to compensate for the extra weight of the new equipment. The engine nacelles had a slightly larger diameter to increase airflow to the engines.

The first unit to receive the NF 13 was No 219 Squadron, based at Kabrit in Egypt during March of 1951. The unit flew night-fighter patrols over some of the most hostile territory in the world at that time and monitored many of the outbursts of trouble between Egypt and Israel. The unit operated the NF 13 for some three years before it disbanded in September of 1954. Many of the aircraft the unit flew would later return to the region when Gloster sold ex-RAF aircraft to nations in the Middle East.

The other RAF unit to fly the NF 13 was No 39 Squadron who received their first aircraft in March of 1953 at Fayid in Egypt. No 39 Squadron would have a longer association with the NF 13 since they kept it in service until the end of the 1950s. They also flew the aircraft in combat, being part of the RAF contingent during the Suez conflict. In 1955, the squadron moved to Malta as part of the RAF's withdrawal from Egypt. They remained on the island until late 1958.

Besides the RAF, the NF 13 was to see service with four other air forces. In Europe, France purchased two aircraft during 1956. These were delivered to the CEV test center, where they were used for test purposes.

This Meteor NF 13 (WM321) of No 219 Squadron carries the squadron badge on the nose. The Meteor was later written off after suffering a mid-air fire during 1954. The squadron markings consisted of two Red chevrons on a Black bar. (JDR Rawlings via R. L. Ward)

This Meteor NF 13 (WM367) was used by the A&AEE until it was declared non-airworthy during 1970. It was sold to Visionair during 1981, but remained at Boscombe Down for some while. Compared to operational squadrons, the aircraft used by the A&AEE were very plainly marked. (J.D.R. Rawlings via R.L. Ward)

The other three operators were all in the Middle East. Syria was the first customer in the region, receiving six ex-RAF aircraft during 1954. They were given serials 471-476 and were used for air defense against night attacks coming from Israel. They did not have a long service career and were replaced by Soviet fighters.

Egypt purchased six ex-RAF aircraft during 1955 and some were ex-No 219 Squadron aircraft. Like the Syrian aircraft, they were used for night air defense, covering Cairo and the Canal Zone from Israeli attacks. The aircraft served throughout the Suez conflict and were later replaced by Soviet-built aircraft.

The third Middle East country to fly the Meteor NF 13 was Israel, who received six aircraft between 1956 and 1958. One of these aircraft was used for a night interception of an Egyptian Il-14 Crate transport, thought to be carrying the Commanding General of the Egyptian Army, General Amar. The aircraft was successfully intercepted and destroyed by a NF 13 of No 119 Squadron, IDF/AF. In the event, it turned out that the aircraft was not carrying the general, since his take off had been delayed and another Il-14 carrying junior officers had proceeded his. It was this aircraft that was intercepted and shot down. The Meteor NF 13 continued to serve in the IDF/AF until 1962, operating along side French Vautour IIN night-fighters.

Meteor NF 14

The last Meteor night-fighter variant was the Meteor NF 14 and it differed from the earlier variants in a number of ways. The prototype NF 14 was a NF 12 (WM261) modified with a three foot longer nose section, a newly designed cockpit with a clear blown rear sliding canopy replacing the side opening framed canopy used on the earlier variants. The lengthened nose was necessary to carry an improved AI radar set that gave the aircraft a far better chances of intercepting the target. The armament of the NF 14 remained the same as all Meteor variant, four 20MM cannon.

Due to the heightened tensions of the Cold War, development of the NF 14 was shrouded in secrecy by the Ministry of Defense and although the prototype made its first flight on 23 October 1953, the first official photos (heavily retouched by the Ministry of Defense) were not released to the press until May of 1954. The official reason for the photographic retouching was that the aircraft had not been painted!

At the time of the press release, the aircraft had already been in service with No 25 Squadron at West Malling for some four months. During that month (May) No 85 Squadron began to re-equip followed the following month by No 152 Squadron. By the end of the year Nos 46 and 264 Squadrons had also taken delivery of their NF 14s. Deliveries then slowed, with two squadrons re-equipping during 1955, one in 1956 and one in 1957. In addition, a night-fighter Operational Conversion Unit (OCU), No 238 OCU, was also outfitted with the NF 14 during 1955.

The NF 14 was a very popular aircraft with its crews and was often referred to by its nickname "Queen of the Skies." Only 100 aircraft were built and its time in service with the RAF was short. None were exported to foreign users, except for two ex-RAF aircraft that were given to the French for test work. The French aircraft were delivered during 1955 and were operated by the CEV from Bretigny along side other Meteor NF variants and were still in service during the mid-1980s.

The RAF began to replace the NF 14 in squadron service with the Javelin as early as February of 1956, when No 46 Squadron traded in its NF 14 and NF 12s for the new all weather fighter. Most were replaced in the UK during the 1958-59 period, although a number remained in service in the Far East.

During early 1959, a refresher course was given to a number of crews at RAF Leeming who were destined for assignment at Tengah, Singapore. These crews would replace returning crews from No 60 Squadron since the unit was changing its role and equipment from day fighter to night-fighter. Tensions were running high in the region because of the Malayan Emergency and No 60 Squadron was to take delivery of a number of NF 14s to provide night-fighter cover to British forces in the area. The unit flew the Meteor NF 14 from Tengah for some two years before receiving Javelins. When No 60 Squadron retired its Meteors, the last front-line Meteor squadron ceased to exist.

Meteor NF (T) 14

Following the replacement of the NF 14 as a front-line fighter, some fourteen aircraft were modified to NF (T) 14 standards by removing the armament and AI radar. The radar unit was replaced by a UHF radio set and the aircraft were assigned to No 2 Air Navigation School at Thorney Island in June of 1959. The role assigned to the aircraft was to train navigators in jet

This Meteor NF 14 (WS810) of No 264 Squadron was on public display during a 1956 Battle of Britain air show. The unit flew both the NF 14 and NF 11. The fuselage markings consisted of Black and Yellow bars. (MAP)

aircraft.

During 1962, the Meteors of No 2 ANS were absorbed by No 1 Air Navigation School and these aircraft continued to give excellent service until replaced by Dominies during 1965.

Following their retirement, most of the NF 14s ended up being scrapped although a few were preserved in museums and three were registered on the British Civil Register. One of these was owned by Rolls-Royce, one by Ferranti and one by Target Towing Aircraft Company. The Ferranti aircraft ended its days in a museum in Scotland, while the other two were last reported during 1969 to be in Senegal.

Fuselage Development

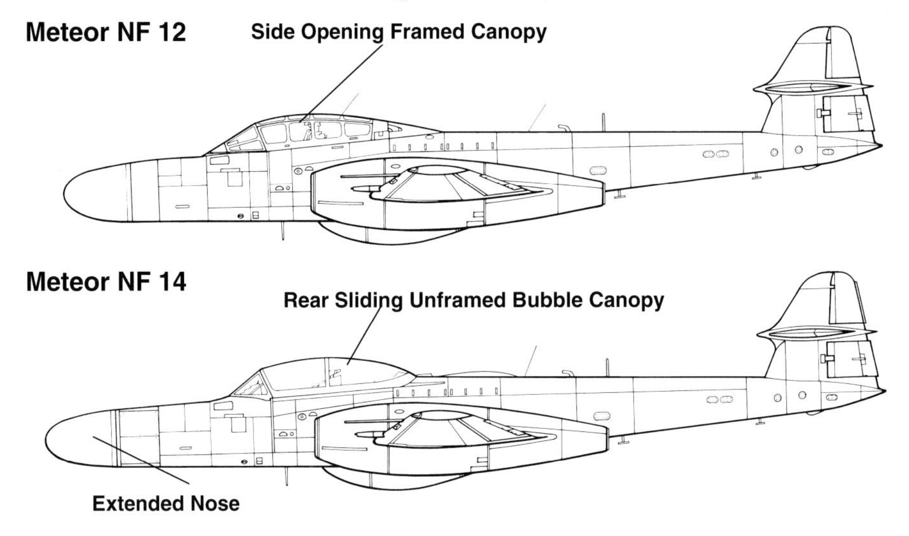

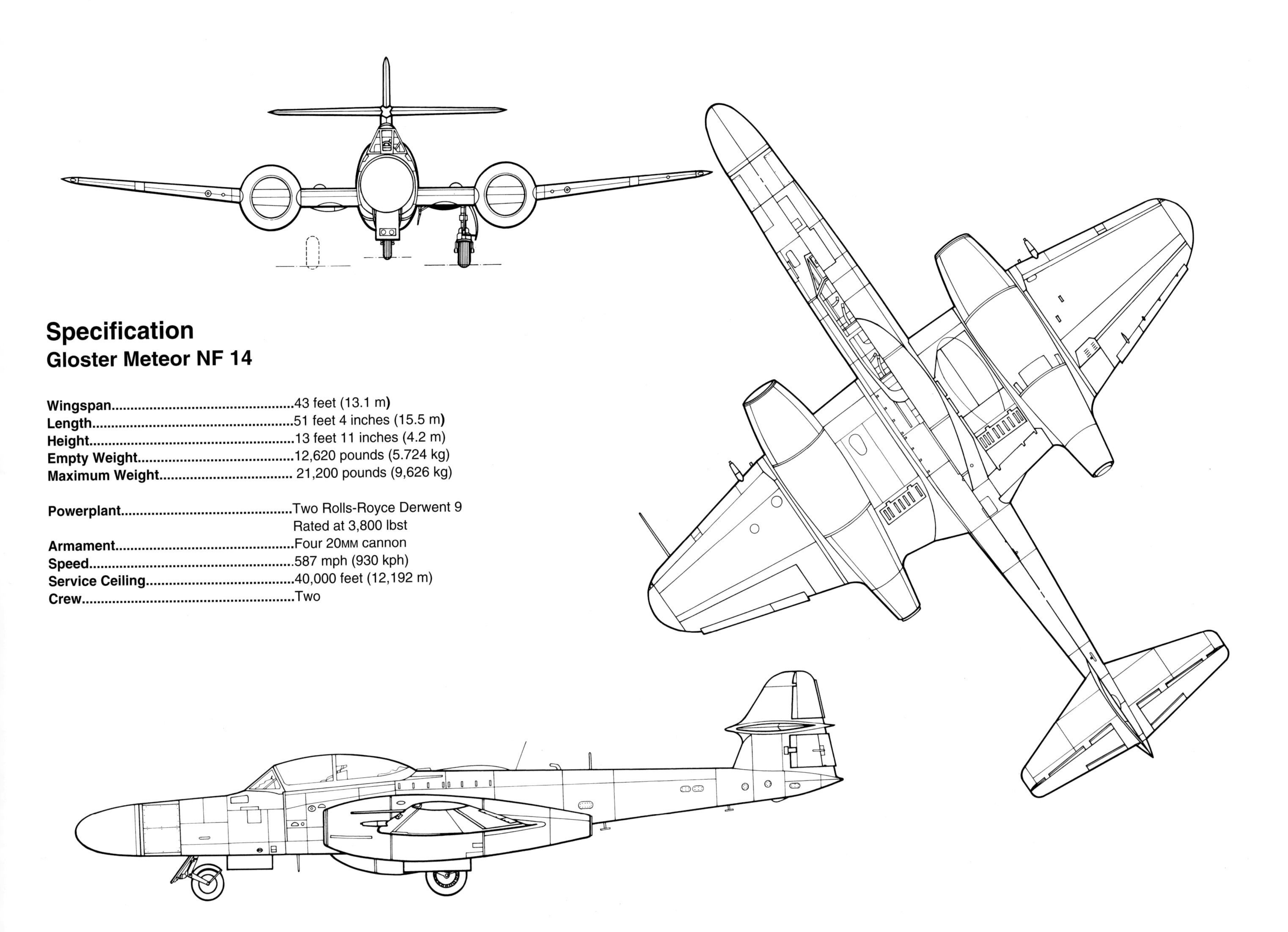

Specification
Gloster Meteor NF 14

Wingspan	43 feet (13.1 m)
Length	51 feet 4 inches (15.5 m)
Height	13 feet 11 inches (4.2 m)
Empty Weight	12,620 pounds (5.724 kg)
Maximum Weight	21,200 pounds (9,626 kg)
Powerplant	Two Rolls-Royce Derwent 9 Rated at 3,800 lbst
Armament	Four 20mm cannon
Speed	587 mph (930 kph)
Service Ceiling	40,000 feet (12,192 m)
Crew	Two

A flight of Nine NF 14s of No 152 Squadron fly in a tight formation. NF 14 crews often referred to their aircraft as "The Queen of the Skies." (Charles Brown/RAF Museum)

This Meteor NF 14 (WS836) of No 64 Squadron carried no unit markings on the fuselage. At this time the unit was based at Duxford. The aircraft in the background is a No 9 Squadron Canberra. (MAP)

The White hexagon and Red/Black checks identify this NF 14 as being assigned to No 85 Squadron. This Meteor appears rather weathered as it prepares for another mission during 1960. (MAP)

This NF 14 of No 152 Squadron was parked in front of the hangars at Wattisham, while undergoing an engine ground run during 1961. Engine access panels on the Meteor were not hinged and to gain access to the engine the panels had to be totally removed. (MAP)

This NF 14 (WS838) was assigned to the All Weather Operational Conversion Unit, Radar Research Establishment and No 64 Squadron before being retired to a Museum at RAF Cosford. (BAe)

A small number of NF 14s were used as dual control trainers and were among the last Meteors in service. This NF(T) 14 (WS789) was overall Silver lacquer with DayGlo stripes. It served with No 1 Air Navigation School until 1965. (MAP)

Martin-Baker Meteors

One of the most unusual roles the Meteor had been used for was the one used by Martin-Baker Ltd. for ejection seat trials. With the development of the ejection seat, over the past forty years, there has been a need for a stable platform with which to test new seat designs. After a number of aircraft were evaluated, Martin-Baker decided that the ideal platform for this work was the Meteor. Shortly after the end of the Second World War Martin-Baker was given a Meteor F 3 (EE416) for use in ejection seat trials. The aircraft was modified with a opening on the fuselage behind the cockpit allowing the installation of the test seat. This aircraft was used for the first airborne ejection seat test, using a dummy, on 14 June 1946. This was followed by several more before the first true ejection with a human subject was made the following month. Bernard Lynch was the guinea pig on that test which was conducted on 24 July 1946. He later went on to make more than thirty other successful ejections.

Two more F 3s were used before the company received their first T 7 during 1952. This aircraft (WA634) was modified to have the test seat in the second cockpit and was used for a number of trials with various marks of seats including the first ground ejection and the first rocket-assisted seat ejection before it was retired. The aircraft now resides in the RAF Museum collection at RAF Cosford.

WA634 was replaced by two other T 7s (WA638 and WL419) which are still operational with the company. Both aircraft are restricted to only flying a few hours per month in order to extend their lives. If there are no tests scheduled, then this reduced flying schedule is not a problem. Both aircraft are maintained in pristine condition by their ground crews which is somewhat amazing, considering that both airframes are far older than the men working on them.

The first aircraft used by Martin-Baker for ejection seat tests was a modified F 3 (HE416) which had a second cockpit to house the seat being tested. The aircraft had an unusual finish, part camouflage and part Silver lacquer. (Martin-Baker)

The first Meteor T 7 dedicated to ejection seat testing was WA634 which was operated by Martin-Baker for many years until it was replaced by two new T 7s. The aircraft now resides in the RAF Museum's collection at RAF Cosford. (Author)

An ejection seat is test fired from the rear cockpit of WL419, one of the Meteor T 7s still serving with Martin-Baker for ejection seat tests. The aircraft is overall Silver lacquer with Red panels. (Martin-Baker)

Combat

The Suez Conflict

In July of 1956 Egyptian President Abdel Nasser nationalized the Suez Canal Company shortly after the last British troops had left the region. Nasser was engaging in "sabre rattling" following the refusal of the British Government to supply Egypt with arms for use against Israel. He then turned to the Soviet Union for aid, which was only too happy to assist the Egyptians, considering this country controlled the canal through which most of the West's oil supplies traveled.

As the British and French realized that Nasser would not be convinced by political pressure, a military plan was drawn up which would be put into action with the aid of Egypt's arch enemy, Israel. An Israeli diversionary movement would draw Egyptian forces away from the canal zone, allowing the British and French to occupy the zone with minimum losses. The first objective was to secure control of the air and to remove the threat of the Egyptian Air Force interference in the operation.

Two squadrons of Meteors were part of the British force, No 39 Squadron, flying NF 13s and No 208 Squadron flying Meteor FR 9s. No 39 Squadron was based at Nicosia on the island of Cyprus with No 208 Squadron being based at Ta Kali on the island of Malta. These units were just a small part of the British forces in the region. The RAF had thirteen Canberra bomber squadrons and four Valiant squadrons deployed to the area, in addition to fighter and strike aircraft and naval aircraft aboard aircraft carriers in the Med. The French supplied fighter and strike aircraft to the operation.

Among the RAF aircraft deployed to the Suez Canal Zone were these Meteor FR 9s of No 205 Squadron. The FR 9s assigned to the squadron flew in a mix of color schemes, some were camouflaged, while others were in overall Silver lacquer. (IWM)

Part of the Egyptian forces that fought against the Anglo-French forces were the Meteors of No 20 Squadron, Royal Egyptian Air Force. These included twelve Meteor F 4s and nine Meteor T 7s. Egyptian T 7s had been modified with underwing rocket rails and were capable of flying operational ground attack sorties. The aircraft were overall Silver lacquer with Green and White markings. (Dr. David Nicolle)

The Egyptian forces facing the Allies included a large number of Soviet types (many of which were not yet combat ready) as well as British types such as Vampire and Meteor fighters. This situation brought out the possibility of the Meteors meeting Meteors in combat. The Egyptian Meteor units were No 20 Squadron based at Deversoir and No 5 Squadron based at Fayid (which was also home to the Fighter Training Unit, which flew both Meteors and Vampires). Both bases were located near the West Bank of the Canal Zone close to the Great Bitter Lake.

One of the first objectives was to destroy as many of the Egyptian airfields as possible. Raids against these were led by Canberras and Valiants and began on 31 October. In response to these night raids, the Egyptians scrambled a number of Meteor NF 13s to try and intercept the bombers. The bomber raids were coming in at 40,000 feet in order to minimize the chances of an interception, but one Egyptian Meteor was able to get in close to a flight of Valiants and open fire. One bomber was damaged before it was able to climb above the Meteor's ceiling.

This appears to have been the only recorded incident of contact between Egyptian Meteors and RAF aircraft during the conflict. The RAF Meteor FR 9s were tasked with flying armed reconnaissance patrols over the waters between Malta and Egypt looking for enemy shipping or any stray enemy aircraft. The NF 13s flew night patrols over Cyprus to prevent the possi-

Meteors were used during many of the periods when Israel's forces were drawn into confrontation with its Arab neighbors. The Meteor F 8 was an excellent aircraft for the ground attack role and this camouflaged Israeli Defense Force/Air Force Meteor saw action in several wars. Upon retirement it was preserved at Hatzerim, as part of the IDF/AF Museum. Its last service days were spent at the Holtz Technical High School in Tel Aviv. (IDF/AF)

bility of a surprise Egyptian attack on the British bases.

Backed by their superior air power, the Allied forces pushed toward the Canal Zone and as they reached this objective, they were forced to withdraw their forces at the request of the United Nations, following the threat of possible nuclear retaliation by the Soviet Union in response to the attack on its Middle Eastern ally. The United States had also threatened financial sanctions against both countries.

During the conflict the RAF lost no Meteors and, although the Egyptians never admitted to any losses, the RAF claimed to have destroyed eleven Meteors of various marks. This was not the last combat for the Egyptian Meteor units. A short time later they would again see action, this time against Israel.

Arab-Israeli Conflicts

Three Middle Eastern nations have operated the Meteor with Israel on one side and Egypt and Syria opposing them as part of the Arab forces surrounding them. All have operated similar Meteor variants, day fighters, night-fighters, reconnaissance-fighters and trainers, in similar numbers, giving an even balance for the type between the three nations.

Egypt was the first to receive the type during 1950, but no contact was made between these fighters and Israeli aircraft. A number of incidents with Egyptian aircraft occurred shortly after the Meteor entered Israeli service. In July of 1954, IDF/AF Meteors attempted to intercept an intruder (an EAF Sea Fury) over Israeli territory. The Sea Fury was able to evade the Meteors and returned unharmed to Egyptian airspace. These types of incursions continued and on 29 August 1955, the first jet vs jet combat took place when a pair of IDF/AF Meteors intercepted four Egyptian Vampires. One Vampire was shot down and another was damaged. Another engagement took place on 1 September 1955, when four EAF Vampires crossed into Israeli territory and were intercepted by a pair of Meteors. One aircraft, a FR 9, successfully

A Meteor NF 13 of the IDF/AF on the ramp at an unidentified Israeli air base during the 1960s. The aircraft was very weathered and carried a unit badge on the fin tip. (J.D.R. Rawlings via R. L. Ward)

This NF 13 had the longest career of any Israeli Meteor. When it was retired from active service, it was retained by the commanding officer of Ramat David Air Base, Colonel Lev, until his death in 1973. It then became 4X-BET engaged in test work for Israel Aircraft Industries until it was handed over to the IDF/AF museum. (IDF/AF)

This IDF/AF Meteor T 7 has had the serial number removed by Israeli censors. The IDF/AF received a total of four Meteor T 7s were exported to Israel all fitted with target towing lugs attached to the rear portion of the underfuselage fuel tank. (IDF/AF)

shot down two Vampires. The same day other IDF/AF Meteors intercepted two EAF Vampires and destroyed one.

The following year saw the Sinai Campaign against Egypt, which was a diversion for the Anglo/French attack on the Suez canal. The IDF/AF had replaced the Meteor in the air-to-air role with the Mystere and the Meteor squadrons were assigned the ground attack role, including a number of T 7s which were armed with underwing rocket rails.

The first mission involving Egyptian Meteors occurred on the afternoon of 30 October 1956, when a flight of two Meteors and six MiG-15s arrived over the Mitla Pass. As the Meteors started their attacks, the MiGs flying top cover were engaged by Israeli Mysteres. The Meteors continued their ground attack while the dogfight took place above them. After the battle, the Meteors returned home. The end result of the fight was one MiG destroyed and one Mystere severely damaged.

During one IDF/AF ground attack sortie, two Meteors were intercepted by a flight of

(Left) The Meteor NF 13 was used by both Egypt and Israel during the 1950s. This Egyptian NF 13 is parked on a desert air strip somewhere in Egypt. (Dr. David Nicolle)

This Egyptian Air Force Meteor F 4 was partially inside a makeshift hangar during the early 1960s. The aircraft carries the later style Red/White/Black national markings of the United Arab Republics Air Force (UARAF) but the retains the Black and White ID bands on the fuselage and wings. (Dr. David Nicolle)

Meteor FR 9s of No 206 Squadron overfly the pyramids near Cairo during the mid-1950s. The aircraft are in a mix of color schemes from overall Silver lacquer to standard RAF day fighter camouflage. (208 Sqn)

Egyptian MiG-15s. One pilot ditched his drop tanks and ran for the safety of his own lines while the other delayed. Only one tank was jettisoned, putting the Meteor off balance and into a spin. Presumably the MiG pilots thought that this would be the end for the Meteor, but somehow he recovered and was able to return to base. Following these battles over and around the Mitla pass, there are no records of further contact between Meteors in any of these nations.

Other Actions

Since the end of the Second World War the Meteor has seen combat in a number of roles and locations, both in RAF and French Air Force service.

Kenya

As part of the RAF detachment involved in the Mau Mau Emergency, two Meteor PR 10s of No 13 Squadron were deployed to Kenya to provide photographic reconnaissance services to British forces making raids on prohibited areas of the country held by the guerrilla group. The aircraft deployed during 1954 and were withdrawn late in 1955.

(Left) This Meteor FR 9 of No 206 Squadron is parked on an airfield in the Middle East, believed to be in Aden. These aircraft flew armed reconnaissance patrols over hostile territory and were extremely useful since they were capable of flying dual role missions, reconnaissance and strike. (208 Sqn)

This PR 10 (WH569) of No 13 Squadron is parked in the scorching sun at Habbaniyah, Iraq during 1958. The unit deployed to several "hotspots" throughout the Middle East providing reconnaissance support for British forces. The aircraft has a power cart plugged in to provide the electrical power needed to start the engines. (MAP)

Aden

With the anti-British feeling running high throughout the Middle East during the 1950s, it came as no surprise when trouble flared in the British protectorate of Aden. In 1954, No 208 Squadron, flying FR 9s, redeployed from Egypt to Khormaksar in Aden. While stationed in Aden the unit flew armed reconnaissance patrols against rebel tribesmen and Yemeni raiding parties who had crossed the border. The aircraft moved to Cyprus for the period of the Suez operation, but returned to Aden once this campaign was completed.

Another FR 9 unit, the Arabian Peninsula Photo Recce Flight,. was formed in the region late in the 1950s. This was later to become No 1417 Flight, responsible for flying reconnaissance missions over a number of important targets in the area, monitoring the vast number of small flare ups that occurred throughout the period.

Cyprus

Shortly before the Suez conflict, there was a small terrorist group intent on driving the

The ground crew of this Meteor FR 9 of No 8 Squadron poses for a group photo somewhere in the Middle East during 1959 while refueling the aircraft. The canopy is probably a replacement since it is unpainted. The fuselage squadron insignia is in (top to bottom) Sand, Red, Blue. The small open circular panel is the external power port. (MAP)

British out of Cyprus. Known as the EOKA, this group started murdering off duty servicemen and bombing British interests on the island. The British reinforced their forces, including Meteor FR 9s of No 208 Squadron, which flew anti-terrorist armed-reconnaissance patrols over the Troodos Mountains, the stronghold of the EOKA. As the RAF was drawn into the conflict over Egypt, the EOKA terrorist found that they could launch their attacks with less interference from the sky. Once the Suez operation had ended, the RAF once more turned their attentions back to offensive patrols against the terrorists. The FR 9s were later joined by NF 13s of No 39 Squadron, with both units carrying out attacks against the mountain strongholds.

Malaya

With the growing threat of Communism in the Far East during the 1950s, the British became faced with a communist insurgency in Malaya. Operating out of the jungle areas of the country, the MRLA insurgents undertook a large number of guerrilla attacks against British interests throughout the country. In December of 1955, No 81 Squadron received its first Meteor PR 10s to replace their aging Mosquitoes. The PR 10s were joined for a short while by a pair of F 8s, that were attached to No 45 Squadron during 1955. The PR 10s flew a great number of reconnaissance missions in support of British air and ground forces engaged in counter-insurgency missions until the Malay Emergency was declared ended in 1960.

Algeria

The French, as well as the British, had troubles in their colonies requiring the deployment of Meteors to the trouble spots. In the North African state of Algeria, a nationalist uprising led to numerous attacks against French forces and interests around the country. French NF 11s of EX N1/71 were used to fly patrols over remote areas searching for Arab terrorists. In addition to patrols, the NF 11s were used for strike missions, but these made little impact on the overall outcome of the conflict.

Test And Trials Aircraft

Throughout its career the Meteor was used for a large number of trials involving engines, radar and other various modifications.

The introduction of a jet fighter into RAF service prompted a great deal of interest from the Royal Navy who were looking at the possibility of operating jets from aircraft carriers. As a result, deck handling trials were held aboard HMS PRETORIA CASTLE during 1945 using the Meteor prototype F9/40. Following these tests, two aircraft were modified for sea trials. They were stripped of all armament and other unnecessary equipment, and the arresting gear from a Sea Hornet was fitted and the landing gear was strengthened to take the higher landing sink rates. In addition, the landing gear doors were removed for fear they might foul the arresting gear.

Following trials on the simulated deck at Boscombe Down the aircraft carried out a number of landings aboard HMS ILLUSTRIOUS and IMPLACABLE during 1948. The trials were a great success and the Navy was reportedly very impressed by the Meteor's performance. In the event, the Meteor was not chosen by the Navy, that service opting for the Supermarine Attacker instead.

A modified Meteor F 3 (EE387) makes a successful deck landing on a Royal Navy aircraft carrier during 1948. Even though the tests were highly successful, the Navy opted for the Supermarine Attacker as its first carrier jet. (Fleet Air Arm Museum)

Trent Meteor

Rolls Royce obtained a Meteor F 1 (EE227) for use in testing of the turboprop RB50 Trent engine. To give the proper ground clearance for the propeller, the Meteor was modified with an extended landing gear and small fins were added to the horizontal stabilizers to increase lateral stability. The new engines were found to fit the existing Meteor nacelles with slight modification. The Trent Meteor was flown for the first time on 20 September 1945, but was found to have very bad handling characteristics. The aircraft was grounded while modifications were made to the length of the propeller blades and further trials were then carried out. With the conclusion of the test program during 1948, the aircraft was scrapped.

Meteors of various marks were used to test a number of engines in order to try to improve the performance of the aircraft, although none made a dramatic improvement in overall performance. Some to the types tested include the Armstrong-Siddeley Sapphire, Rolls-Royce Avon, Nene and SNECMA Atar.

(Right) The Trent Meteor was used by Rolls Royce for tests with the first turboprop engine, the RB50 Trent. The modified aircraft was found to be very unstable. The test aircraft was a modified Meteor F 1 (EE227). (Charles Brown/RAF Museum)

The greatly increased length of the engiine nacelles is evident on this Meteor F 8 used to test the Armstrong Siddeley Sapphire engines. The tests did not reveal any great increase in the Meteor's the performance and the project was cancelled. (MAP)

This Meteor F 4 (RA 491) also had modified engine nacelles marking it as an engine test bed. The aircraft was used by Rolls-Royce to test the Avon engine. (MAP)

The British were not the only ones to use the Meteor for test purpose. This NF 11 was operated by the CEV in France for radar tests. The aircraft was the fifth NF 11 delivered to France during the mid-1950s. (MAP)

This Meteor NF 11 was used by the Radar Research Establishment for trials with a number of different radar units. The collical nose cone fitted here was used when the aircraft undertook trials with the radar that was to be fitted to the TSR 2 strike aircraft. The aircraft was finally scrapped for spares during 1982. (MAP)

Tugs And Drones

When its career as a front-line fighter began to end, the Meteor found itself put into service for a number of second line duties.

The aircraft was found to be ideal for the role of aerial target towing and some the the first to be modified for this role were flown by the Royal Navy. Nearly forty Meteor NF 11s were converted to the target towing role under the designation TT 20. A wind driven winch was mounted on the starboard wing inboard of the engine nacelle and this was used to deploy and retrieve the target which was carried under the lower fuselage. The aircraft used in this role towed aerial targets for Royal Navy anti-aircraft gunners and had their undersurfaces painted in bright Yellow with diagonal Black stripes. The TT 20 entered service with the Fleet Air Arm during 1958 at several Naval Air Stations and with the civil company, Airwork, which had a towing contract with the Royal Navy. These aircraft continued in service until 1967.

A few TT 20s were operated by the RAF, being flown by 3/4 Civilian Anti-Aircraft Co-operation Unit at Exeter from 1962 until their retirement during 1970.

Six Meteor NF 11s were converted to the target towing role by Armstrong Whitworth for the Danish Air Force. These aircraft were serialed 508, 512, 517 and 519. The aircraft were owned by the air force, but operated by a civil firm under contract. They were overall Silver lacquer with Red bands around the rear fuselage, nose and wingtips.

Four TT 20s were flown by Swedair who flew target towing operations for the Swedish Air

Target Towing Installation

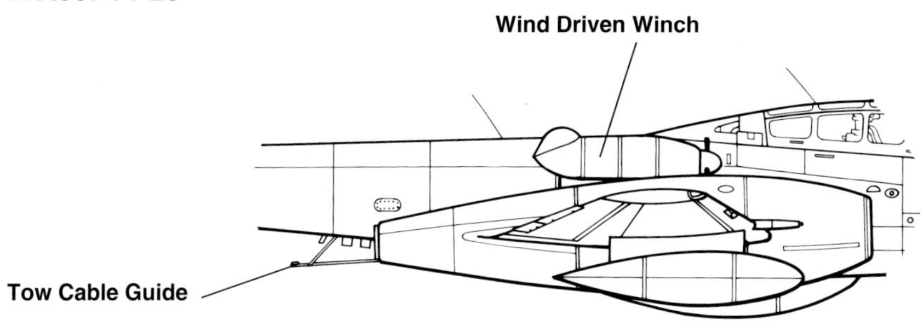

This is one of the two surviving Meteor U 16s (ex-Meteor F 8) still operated by the RAF at Llanbedr in Wales. After serving as a fighter with two RAF squadrons the aircraft was modified in 1991 to drone standards. The aircraft was finished in a high visibility Red and Yellow color scheme. (Author)

The lower fuselage target towing cable guide and target attachment point are visible on the Meteor TT 20 (ex-NF 11) of the Royal Navy Fleet Air Arm. The aircraft was flown by No 728 Squadron at Akrotiri during 1959. This aircraft was later sold to France during 1974. (MAP)

Force under contract. These aircraft flew along side a number of Douglas Skyraiders and three modified Meteor T 7s. The aircraft were painted overall Yellow with Red bands and carried civil registrations. They remained active until the late 1960s, when they were retired and passed to a German company.

With an increasing reliance on air-to-air missiles and surface-to-air missiles, it became apparent that a high performance aerial target was needed to test new weapons. It was felt that surplus Meteors would make ideal targets in that they could climb, dive and bank. A total of ninety-four Meteor F 4s were converted to the target role under the designation U 15. These aircraft had additional radios installed, an automatic pilot, and wingtip camera pods for recording missile behavior. These pods could be automatically or radio command ejected before missile impact, if the target was to be destroyed in the test. In order to make the targets highly visible and easy to track by recording cameras, they were painted in a Red and Yellow color scheme. Twenty aircraft were delivered to RAF Llanbedr in Wales while the remainder went to the Woomera Weapons Research Establishment in Australia.

As the numbers of U 15s decreased a number of Meteor F 8s were modified with a similar equipment fit under the designation U 16 (later redesignated D 16). Some 108 F 8s were modified and used in a similar role as the earlier U 15. At least two of these remain at Llanbedr and it is hoped that these may be saved and preserved.

This TT 20 of the Fleet Air Arm was a rebuilt and converted NF 11 night-fighter. The wind driven wench was mounted above the wing and the target attachment point/cable guide was mounted on the fuselage underside. The TT 20s carried Black diagonal stripes painted across the underside of the aircraft to make them more visible to the gun crews during firing practice. This aircraft of No 728 Squadron, Fleet Air Arm was based at Hal Far, Malta during 1958. (Fleet Air Arm Museum)

Sweden operated a number of T 7s and TT 20s in the target towing role under contract to the Swedish Air Force. This T 7 was painted in overall Yellow with Red trim with the civil registration being carried on the fuselage and under the wings in Black. Originally, this aircraft had served as the prototype of the Gloster Reaper, an unsuccessful ground attack design. It was later converted to T 7 standards and finally to the target towing configuration. After being retired from active service, the aircraft was preserved in Sweden. (Flygvapenmuseum)

Surviving Meteors

A number of Meteors have been preserved as Gate Guardians by several air forces around the world and others are part of museum collections, usually representing the first jet fighter flown by that nation.

For several years the RAF maintained a Meteor T 7 and Vampire T 11 for air shows and displays. These were known as the "Vintage Pair" display team and toured the United Kingdom. They were finished in overall Gray and operated by the Central Flying School. Due to the age of the aircraft and the difficulty in obtaining spares, a ceiling was placed on the number of displays they could perform each year, with the figure being set at fifty. Additionally, strict limits were placed on the types of maneuvers that could be performed and the pilots were cautioned not to overstress the airframes. Unfortunately, both aircraft were lost during a show at RAF Mildenhall. They collided and crashed in a wooded area just outside the base, killing both crews and totally destroying the aircraft.

Adrian Gjertsen, a British aircraft restorer, has added a Meteor NF 11 to his private air force. This aircraft (WM167) had previously served with No 228 Operational Conversion Unit before being converted to TT 20 standard. Following its retirement, the aircraft was rebuilt back to NF 11 standard and painted in the colors of No 141 Squadron.

Another Meteor TT 20 was reported to be on the U.S. Civil Register, owned by Mr. Al Letcher at Mojave, California.

This is the last flying Meteor NF 11 (WM167) owned by Jet Heritage in the United Kingdom. The aircraft was formerly operated as a TT 20 before being restored back to NF 11 standards. It now makes regular appearances at air shows and is to be joined later by a Meteor F 8 currently under restoration. (Adrian Gjertsen)

This Meteor F 8 (WH791) served with a number of RAF units before ending its days in the colors of the unit that first operated the fighter, No 601 Squadron. The aircraft is painted in overall Light Gray with Red and Black squadron marking and is on display at RAF Kemble. (B. Kedward)

The Royal Air Force "in action"

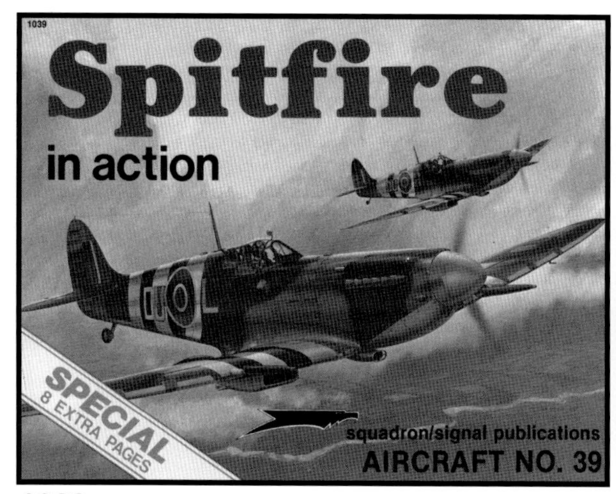

1039

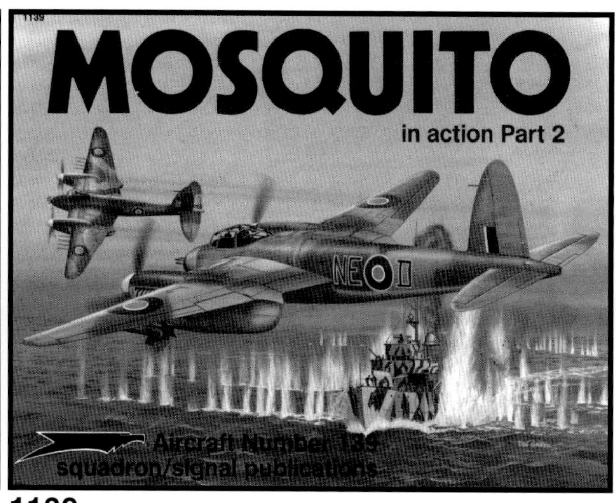

1139

1121